THE EIGHTH PASSENGER

THE EIGHTH PASSENGER

a flight of recollection and discovery

Miles Tripp

WORDSWORTH EDITIONS

First published in Great Britain in 1969
by William Heinemann Ltd.
Revised edition published 1993
by Pen & Sword Books Ltd.

This edition published 2002
by Wordsworth Editions Limited
Cumberland House, Crib Street, Ware,
Hertfordshire SG12 9ET

ISBN 1 84022 252 2

Printed and bound in Great Britain
by Mackays of Chatham plc, Chatham, Kent.

This book is dedicated with affection to

GEORGE KLENNER D.F.C. (pilot and captain)

GEORGE BELL D.F.M. (wireless operator)

HARRY McCALLA (rear gunner)

RAY PARKE (flight engineer)

PAUL SONGEST (mid-upper gunner)

LES WALKER D.F.M. (navigator)

CONTENTS

PREFACE TO NEW EDITION   xi

INTRODUCTION   1

PART ONE

IT'S A GREAT LIFE IF YOU DON'T WEAKEN

1   Marriage Market   9

2   A Debut to Forget   17

3   Home and Faraway   29

4   The Beginning of Fear   37

5   Witten   45

6   The Lost Operations   49

7   Diversions   57

8   The Fault of the English Weather   68

9   The Bombing of Dresden   77

10 The Test   87

11 What the Hell are We Fighting For?   93

12 'This is Good-bye to Able'   102

13 Dig's Day   110

CONTINUED –

PART TWO

A WIND FROM THE PAST

1 The Search Begins   119

2 Harry   129

3 George   134

4 Les   139

5 'Dig'   145

6 Ray   153

7 Paul   160

8 'Mike'   167

9 A Summing-up   171

EPILOGUE   183

NOTES   189

PREFACE TO NEW EDITION

WHEN THIS BOOK was reissued in 1985 it contained an epilogue which dealt with some operational material which had come to hand since first publication in 1969. The epilogue also referred to a crew reunion which was organized for the purpose of a German television documentary on the Dresden raid, as well as matter on LMF (Lack of Moral Fibre) which affected those members of aircrew who could no longer tolerate the continuous stress of facing death every time they flew over enemy occupied Europe.

During the quarter of a century since this book was written I have received many letters and had access to some information which was not available for inclusion in the 1985 epilogue. The mixture of objective and subjective in that epilogue is no longer entirely satisfactory. Accordingly, this new edition contains an appendix with notes, referred to numerically in the text, dealing principally with bombing raids and operational life. Post-war events of a more personal nature relating to my former crew and myself are now contained in a new, shorter epilogue.

There is much I should like to add about the controversial policy of area bombing implemented by Sir Arthur Harris, which policy has been adversely criticized and its effects detrimentally exploited by those intent on minimizing the attempts of Bomber Command to finish a war in which combatants and civilians on both sides were suffering.

But these are matters for another time, a different book.

THE EIGHTH PASSENGER

Overleaf –
Map – Operational Targets
in Western Europe

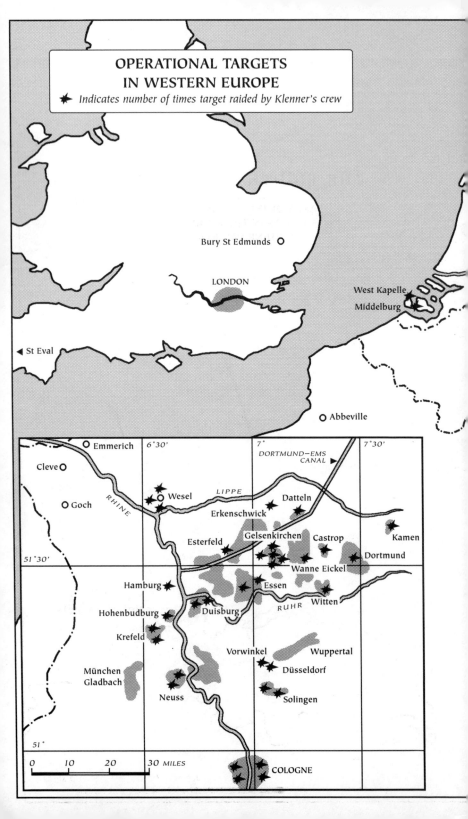

OPERATIONAL TARGETS IN WESTERN EUROPE

✷ Indicates number of times target raided by Klenner's crew

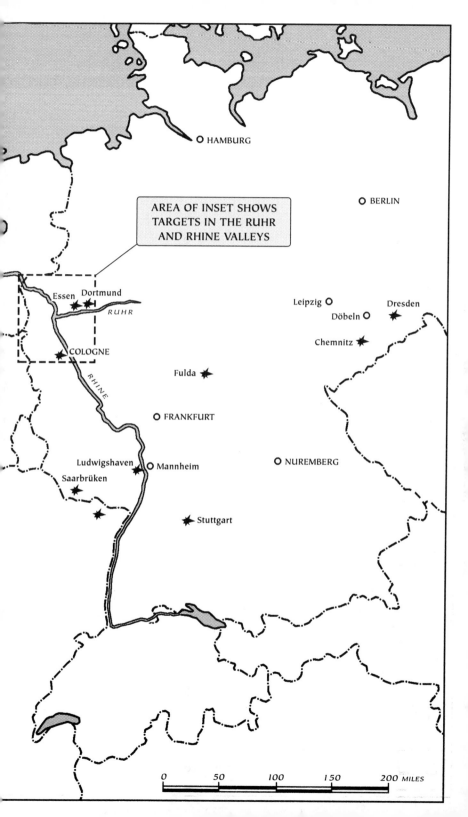

O HAMBURG

O BERLIN

AREA OF INSET SHOWS
TARGETS IN THE RUHR
AND RHINE VALLEYS

Essen Dortmund

RUHR

Leipzig O   Dresden ✳
Döbeln O
✳
Chemnitz ✳

COLOGNE

RHINE

Fulda ✳

O FRANKFURT

O NUREMBERG

Ludwigshaven ✳ O Mannheim
Saarbrüken
✳

✳ Stuttgart

0   50   100   150   200 MILES

Introduction

PETER JONES is an optician whose escape from the routine of his job is to wander through the sky just as his father, and all his forefathers, might have taken a stroll through the woods. It was during the summer of 1967 that I asked Peter if I might fly as his passenger. We were both aware, although the point was not made, of his comparative inexperience as a pilot. He had logged about forty hours solo which is not much compared with the twelve thousand hours or so of an airline captain. He didn't know that I hoped, by flying with him, to master finally a fear which had been with me for more than twenty years.

Late on a fine summer afternoon we drove from his consulting-rooms in London's West End to a small grass airfield at Stapleford Tawney in Essex. He hired a Piper Cherokee, a monoplane powered by a single engine and, side by side, we bumped over the turf and wobbled aloft.

Almost at once he drew my attention to a water-tower and said it was a good landmark, and his voice was smooth with the satisfaction of a man who knows that landmarks are among the rewarding things of life.

A few seconds later he said, 'I don't reckon you can beat this.' I made no reply. 'Are you enjoying it?' he asked.

'Sure,' I said.

We were flying above a carpet of soft greens which was gradually being split by the broadening gleam of a river. Then he said, 'Care to take over for a bit?'

He was handing me my pride and I gripped the stick like a man trying to strangle a snake. In this moment of personal truth I didn't trust my instincts to keep the aircraft level and fixed my gaze on the artificial horizon, the airspeed indicator, and the altimeter. But even in the enormous concentration of flying a Piper Cherokee in broad daylight I was aware of being in thick cloud and the words 'Nose up' repeated themselves compulsively in the fearful silences of my mind.

I held the stick for about two minutes of chronological time (many hours of psychological time) and then said, 'She's yours, Peter.' I'd had enough.

When he had taken control I allowed myself the luxury of recollection and remembered the day, half a lifetime behind, when a pilot had said, 'I'm busting for a slash. Will you take over?' He had been a tough laconic Australian called 'Dig' and simply on the strength of knowing that I had logged a few hours dual on a pilot's course before being washed out he was willing to place his life, and the lives of the rest of the crew, into my failed hands.

I had, indeed, in imagination anticipated a night of horror over Berlin when, mortally wounded, Dig would be dragged from the controls and I would fly a damaged Lancaster back to England and make a brilliant emergency landing thereby earning the Victoria Cross, but I had never imagined that anyone's moment of glory could be heralded by the overfull bladder of a pilot on a training flight. It had been one of those critical occasions when one must go forward or for ever sink into the mire of lost opportunity. I knew that if I had said, 'I can't do it' I should have lost Dig's respect, the respect of the crew and, most important, my self-respect. So I changed places with him and while he went aft to the Elsan I flew a Wellington in thick cloud at seventeen thousand feet over the North Sea.

I have no idea how long we pitched blindly through the sky like a powerful fly piercing a shroud of white cobweb but eventually Dig came back. Physically I felt worn out but a watchful little gargoyle on the Gothic subconscious must have nodded approval because I knew that something had been proved. Alas, that 'something' seemed to need eternal proof; no sooner was it proved than it had to be proved again, like a theorem which always ended Q.E.F. when every emotion craved the absolution of Q.E.D.

The Piper Cherokee passed over Osea Island and flew towards the Mersea Flats. Below, small ships were like bright splashes of paint on a panel of glass.

'Clacton's over there,' said Peter, pointing ahead and to the left.

When we reached the town he said, 'Let's go out to sea.'

2

A couple of minutes later he said, 'Let's go down and get a better view.' He pushed the stick forward and the monoplane roared down.

'That was steeper than I meant,' he said, pulling the stick back.

As we circled over the darkening sea, sinking lower and lower, I didn't relive my life as drowning men are reputed to, but I was vaguely aware that a significant point in time had been reached. Not only was this the day of the summer solstice and the sun fractionally nearer than at any time during the year, and not only were we turning on to the course for home, but I was on the verge of some sort of opportunity.

Peter straightened the Cherokee into level flight and we flew almost due west, towards clouds that were golden with the diffused light of the setting sun. The sky was bright with confidence and I wanted very much to take the controls again.

For a few minutes I flew on a heading of 278 degrees, my eyes flicking from the compass to the glow ahead and the deepening green below. The low sun made it difficult to see directly ahead but eventually we found the water-tower and later began a landing circuit.

As we drove home in his car I mentioned how, after finishing wartime flying in Lancaster bombers, I had been frightened of travelling as a passenger in much safer civilian aircraft. It was a fear that had only been subdued by setting out to fly (when the money was available) on a number of long-distance trips in a variety of aircraft. The flight in the Cherokee had been the latest effort to nail anxieties of which I was slightly ashamed and it had been successful.

Peter came in for a drink when we reached my home and I bragged to my wife about having flown the Cherokee. She said, 'Isn't it funny that letter came today. Today.'

By the morning post a letter had arrived from someone in Birmingham who said he was an authority on Lancaster aircraft. He had tracked down every Lancaster which had flown in the war, and had corresponded with 'several thousand former air and ground crew types'. He was making a record of all operational flights.

I showed the letter to Peter and for a while we talked about coincidences, and how one could dismiss them as flukes or accept them as signposts. Is it merely a curiosity about the unknown, combined with a sense of self-importance, that makes it more attractive to believe that a coincidence, however minuscule when related to the world at large, is nevertheless an indication that there is some sort of purpose in human existence and we are not merely chemical accidents jerking in spasms between meaningless voids?

I wondered if the man who had written to me and signed his letter 'Mike Garbett' was one of those sad self-parodies who sit on bar stools up and down the country, gazing bemusedly at a pint of bitter, and whose handlebar moustaches begin to twitch when someone starts talking about the war. Then, as in a million stage and television skits, the moustaches are caressed by fingers that once rolled a Spit off the top, or diced in a Hallibag at twenty 'thou' and a voice which had once come through crisply over R/T with the gen that there were bandits at angels eleven, but is now slurred with limning the same anecdotes countless times, begins an incantation of place-names – Hamburg, Berlin, Cologne, Essen, Frankfurt – to which the listener, if he is kind, will listen without mockery, for the man who speaks is someone whose present and future was spent, and overspent, where the winds never blow warm.

I invited Mike Garbett to come and have lunch one day and from the moment he stepped out of his car it was obvious that he was not a relic of the war. It transpired that he had been only two years old when the Few lived their legend and his daily occupation was project engineer on fork-lift trucks. Having found from experience that people are suspicious of single-minded enthusiasm where there is no monetary reward, he quickly established his credentials by reeling off a list of squadron locations, commanding officers, pilots and Lancaster airframe numbers.

He had assisted in the preparation of the book *Lancaster, the Story of a Bomber*, and asked which Lancaster my crew had usually flown. To the reply 'A-Able' he said that this was PD277. He then gave the information that the total production of Lancasters, including those manufactured after the war, was 7,374. Of this total no fewer than 3,349 had been lost in action. The figure didn't surprise me. I had heard that nearly half the men who flew as Bomber Command aircrew had been killed in action.

Mike Garbett was collecting material for histories of various squadrons and what made my squadron of special interest was the difficulty in obtaining information on personnel and raids flown. After lunch he copied entries from my log-book and asked whether I had kept in touch with the crew. He wasn't surprised to learn that I knew of the whereabouts of only one member, the Jamaican rear-gunner; the other five had vanished completely. After all, twenty-three years had gone by.

We talked late into the afternoon and after he had gone I started to wonder about the crew, and how each one was faring, and I decided to set down as factually as possible an account of our life together. It would be necessary to write this before attempting to trace the crew so that the narrative would remain uncoloured by their opinions or recollections. Fortunately I still had many notes and records kept at the time or made shortly after the event, and the first part of this book is therefore a fairly documentary account of bombing operations as seen by a Flight-Sergeant bomb-aimer. The second part is about a search for missing persons to find out whether they looked back on the bombing of Germany with nostalgia. Had they been as afraid at the time as I? Were they much different in middle-age from what they had been in youth? Had operational flying taken any physical or psychological toll? With the world in its present mess, did they think our effort had been worth while? And what did they think, twenty years after the event, about the bombing of Dresden? Did they feel any guilt because we had knowingly bombed a civilian population?

It would not only be a search for missing persons; I was also seeking the answers to questions which could not have been asked in the days when we had lived and flown together. But, as is often the way when a man goes searching, whether it is for a religion, a lost tribe or the meaning of hieroglyphs on stone, he ends not only by achieving the object of his quest but also by discovering something of himself. And so it was with me.

It only remains to add that having joined the R.A.F. with blurred and largely emotional motives, not least of which was the youthful behavioural cliché of needing to prove oneself, I found myself on the eve of a posting to an Operational Training Unit at Wing in Buckinghamshire wondering what sort of a crew I should team up with, and whether it would be possible to slip home for a few hours to celebrate my twenty-first birthday.

PART ONE

IT'S A GREAT LIFE IF YOU DON'T WEAKEN

1. *Marriage Market*

ON THE FIRST day men were sent to a large hangar and told it was up to them to form crews among themselves; those who were too sensitive, diffident or withdrawn to respond to these conditions would eventually be crewed up with others of similar temperament. This arbitrary collision of strangers was basically a marriage market and yet the choice of a good flying partner was far more important than a good wife. You couldn't divorce your crew, and you could die if one of them wasn't up to his job at a critical moment.

I felt like a girl at her first dance and cringed at the thought of being a wallflower. Groups of pilots, navigators, wireless operators and air gunners stayed with their own kind but as the morning passed men from each group began to circulate and a jocular insecurity pervaded the cheerless hangar. Every so often one would hear a happy cry, 'Hey, Bill, I've found a navigator!' and if the speaker was an air gunner one readily understood his joy because, although everyone in a bomber crew took the same risk, there was a wage differential between navigators and gunners that created an unacknowledged but undeniable status distinction.

The day dragged by and when the time came to close the hangar I was still a wallflower. That evening I went to the village, had a few drinks and sat down to play the pub piano. A sergeant navigator with a pint of beer in his hand came and stood by the piano. After a while he offered to buy me a drink. Like me he was uncrewed. I duly bought him a return drink and we agreed to team up. He was from the north, aged twenty-one, and his name was Jack.

On the following day Jack came to me greatly excited. He had found a pilot who had already crewed up with a wireless operator. The four of us met. The pilot, a tall, lean Australian Flight Sergeant with blue eyes and a thin pale face, was the same age as Jack. The

9

wireless operator, who wasn't yet twenty, was a hefty good-looking lad from Leeds. Both were named George. It was accepted without any discussion that we should join forces; the only problem was that it might be confusing to have two Georges in the same crew. In the end it was agreed that we should call the pilot 'Dig'. When asked my name I said it was Miles but most R.A.F. friends called me 'Mike'. 'Mike'll do for us,' said Dig.

Late in the nineteenth century Dig's grandparents had emigrated from Germany and settled in Australia and although he made a joke about bombing the land of his forefathers he spoke very little about his background. During the next few days I tried very hard, perhaps too hard, to know him better, and was uneasily fascinated by the lack of *rapport* between us. Dig was everything I wasn't — tough, mechanically minded, contemptuous of the Arts, a lover of slapstick, loyal and courageous. He had, he told me, a sheila in Perth who was a beaut, and because he was the first Australian I had ever heard I mistook his fair dinkum slang for poetic imagery. But it soon became apparent that the only close point of contact between us was that I could play *I haven't said Thanks for that Lovely Week-End* and this tune reminded him of his sheila. When I began to sing he asked me whether it hurt me as much to sing as it hurt him to listen.

George, the wireless operator, was very keen to fly on operations. He had taken a signals course with the Air Training Corps and when he had reached the minimum age, seventeen and a half, he had volunteered for aircrew duties. Although he didn't think I talked posh and I didn't think he was a bai-goom Yorkshireman I believe we were both slightly conscious of differences which went beyond accent, and we had few interests in common, although once again I found that the piano was a friend indeed. George's favourite tunes were *Paper Doll* and *It Could Happen to You*, but I think that if we had been travelling in the same train, instead of singing in the Mess, we should have retired behind newspapers after a few moments of polite conversation.

One day Dig informed us that he had got a brace of gunners and therefore the crew was complete until we reached Conversion Unit when we should be allocated a flight engineer. The gunners, Paul and Harry, had already agreed that Paul would man the mid-upper turret and Harry would be 'Tail-end Charlie' in the rear turret. Harry had a brown skin, high cheekbones and an arrogant bearing; it was not difficult to imagine that the Scottish seafarers and African women among his ancestors were proud clansmen and the daughters of tribal chiefs.

Occasionally he would adopt a mannered way of speaking and embellish subordinate clauses with ironical euphemisms to such effect that the listener would become lost in a maze of nineteenth-century diplomatic English. Of one somewhat plain member of the Women's Auxiliary Air Force he remarked, 'It is to be doubted if anyone could with justification state that here was a flower born to blush unseen and waste its sweetness on the desert air.' But while he could appreciate delicacy and nuance in conversation, he could also swear hard and fight. At this time there were very few West Indians in England and, of these, only a handful were in aircrew. During the entire period of training in Bomber Command, and later when on a squadron, we did not see or meet another West Indian flyer. Harry was twenty-four and the old man of the crew.

The other gunner, Paul, had been born in Aberdeen of English parents but most of his life had been spent in Liverpool and he possessed the lively eyes and slightly undernourished look of a typical Liverpudlian. He was the smallest man in the crew and sometimes called 'Junior'. He loved danger and to say that a man was a crazy bastard was about the highest praise he could bestow. He laughed a lot but spoke sparingly, usually in short, clipped sentences. Everyone liked Paul; he was game for anything, hardly ever complained, and was against nothing and nobody except bullshit and authority. He preferred gambling at cards to taking a chance with a woman, and he drank heavily.

Dig brought the six of us together in the Sergeants' Mess and ceremoniously bought six pints of beer with which to toast our future success. While we were drinking, another Australian pilot came across. 'You blokes got him,' he said, looking at Dig. 'I tell you. When we were at S.F.T.S. I was the only bugger with the nerve to formate on him.'

Dig bellowed with laughter. 'Don't take any notice of young Gog,' he said. 'Gog doesn't know his arse from a hole in the ground.' He glanced at us affectionately. 'I've got the best bloody crew in Bomber Command,' he said.

I admired his confidence. At this stage we had not been on a single flight together. But soon we were on our way. While Jack remained at base to gain navigational experience, flying with senior crews, the rest went with Dig to a satellite aerodrome so that he could practice circuits and bumps on a Wellington. Jack didn't like being left behind but was consoled by the thought of seeing his fiancée at the week-end. She had just become pregnant and they wanted to accelerate plans for the wedding.

We said good-bye to Jack and the next news we had of him was that he was dead. He had been inside a Wellington which had blown up on its landing approach.

A gloom fell over us but Jack's fiancée must have felt utter despair. We didn't know her name, or where she lived, and, although it might have been a nice gesture to seek her out, condolences are merely an acknowledgement of sorrow, they do not palliate grief.

It was an exciting moment when Dig took off for the first time without an instructor on board and, to prove that we were on our own and could do as we liked, George, contrary to regulations, tuned in to the Forces programme, and for a while dance music played over the intercom.

Then we were allocated a new navigator. Les, a pale-faced, lanky youth from Sheffield, had been a clerk in a builder's office before joining the R.A.F. He was diffident and shy and a neglected remainder in the marriage market. For a man of his temperament it must have been painfully embarrassing to join a crew who had lost their previous navigator in tragic circumstances, and if he was made to feel at home almost immediately this was entirely due to Dig's insistence that he had the best crew and, if Les was in it, then he must be the best navigator.

Nor was Dig's confidence shaken by Les's failure to find the right target in a ground exercise called a 'grope' which was designed to simulate operational conditions in a lofty, darkened room. Twenty minutes after the other crews had bombed Wuppertal, Les was bombing an unmarked area near Aachen. By the time he had navigated his aircraft back to England the other crews had left for lunch.

A fierce argument followed between Dig, who was a mere Flight Sergeant, and the instructor who held the rank of Flight Lieutenant. The instructor wanted to hold Les back for further training and to give us another replacement, but Dig refused to accept this suggestion. One couldn't help admiring Dig for his stand but I knew that if I had been in his position I would have accepted the instructor's offer. The difference between us, and it is discreditable to me, was that Dig was a born leader with a leader's sense of team loyalty and I was a man for whom self-preservation was ultimately more important than any loyalty.

During the next few weeks we flew as a crew. Dig quickly became bored with night flying exercises and would ask me to take over while he went to the back of the aircraft to lie down and sleep. This helped me to know and work better with Les, because I would fly for as long as three hours on the courses he gave, but sometimes I worried about having a sleep-prone pilot. How would we fare on operations, I wondered, if he was constantly yawning and talking of taking a kip.

The mishaps which befell most crews occurred to ours. There was the time when our aircraft landed with less than ten gallons in its tanks; the time when anti-aircraft defences near Stratford-upon-Avon opened fire on us; the time when Dig set the altimeter one thousand feet too high and it was Harry's keen night vision that detected we were skimming hedges and treetops; the time I tried to teach Paul about bomb-aiming and he dropped a practice bomb so far from the authorized area that it fell beside the main line from Euston to Crewe; and the time I tried to map-read the way to my home only thirty miles from base when we should have been air-testing a Wellington, failed to find it, and, without a navigator on board, then failed to find base. We were lost for nearly two hours. Then we were posted to Conversion Unit so that Dig could learn how to handle four-engined aircraft.

We were joined by the seventh and last crew member. He was just nineteen years old but had been top of his course as flight engineer and possibly he had been delegated to our crew to improve our level of performance. His name was Ray, he came from a village in Norfolk, and it had been his childhood ambition to keep goal for the

Norwich Canaries. Ray and I enjoyed a natural animosity from the start. He had close-cropped hair; mine was long. He had no time for music and literature; I sneered at technical know-how. He would spend an evening polishing and sweeping his bedspace; the ration of coal was stored under my bedspace where it was reckoned safe from theft by other crews. In general, he was as intolerant of arty-crafty types as I was of swede bashers. We were destined to form a love-hate relationship in which the love was derisory.

Another training mishap, less typical than the others, befell the crew one afternoon when returning from a navigational exercise which had been delayed. Dig began glancing at his watch. He had a date with a WAAF and had yet to shave and change into his best blue; the time for his date was less than twenty minutes away as we approached the airfield. I went to sit beside him to put down the wheels, advance throttles and let down the flaps (the bomb-aimer's task on Stirlings) but when the aircraft was fifty feet from the ground it was obvious that a landing on the short runway was impossible. I expected Dig to order overshoot procedure, but he said nothing; his jaw was set and each whisker bristled with the determination to meet his girl-friend on time.

The wheels touched down half-way along the runway and at the same moment I pulled back the throttles, trying to strangle life from the engines. But in spite of this, and Dig's attempts to brake, the Stirling careered past the concrete runway end, bumped over rough ground, crashed through a hedge and hit a ditch. The undercarriage collapsed and the port wing broke while its revolving airscrews churned up turves. I was thrown upwards and my head banged the cockpit cover; Dig seemed to slide away beneath me.

The hazard of exploding petrol tanks and the fire made me move fast. I wrenched back the cockpit cover, clambered out and dropped to the ground. Dig followed, but there was no explosion and luckily no one had been hurt apart from minor cuts and bruises. Dig had to forego his date; the Commanding Officer wished to see him.

He came away from the interview looking remarkably cheerful. He had been told that his commission had come through on that very morning and his only punishment was to be a red ink endorsement in his log-book and the withholding of promulgation of his promotion until he was due to leave the unit. Considering that the Stirling was a total wreck, and had to be written off as scrap, this was generous treatment. Harry was not so fortunate. To his bewilderment he was charged with not being in his correct crew position, the tail turret, during the landing. He was taken under escort to the Commanding Officer and the rest of us went to the Mess to wait for him. Eventually he re-appeared, his head held high and his face taut with well-bred disdain.

There was a chorus: 'How did it go, Harry?'...'What happened?'

'He asked what I had to say in answer to the charge, and I told him! I said "God, man, if I'd stayed in my turret I'd be dead! And because I'm not dead, *you charge me!*" '

'What did he say to that?' everyone asked.

'He dismissed the charge,' said Harry.

Dig was not chastened by the experience but he was growing fed up with the craze for playing bridge which had developed among the crew and was being carried to the extent of playing rubbers during day flying exercises. George, Les, Paul and Harry would all squeeze into the navigator's compartment leaving Ray to look after the engines from a position half-way down the aircraft, and Dig and me in the pilot's cabin. One day Dig winked and mouthed the words 'Hold tight'. He pulled the control column into the pit of his stomach and the Stirling's nose reared up. The airspeed dropped to 90 m.p.h. and the aircraft shuddered on the brink of a stall; then Dig pushed the stick forward and gave full right rudder. The Stirling dived and began to roll. He slammed on the opposite rudder and heaved back the stick so that the aircraft soared out of its dive with an awful drag in the opposite direction. Cards floated out of the navigator's compartment like a flock of doves and Les's anxious face appeared. Dig was almost sick with laughter as the Stirling bucked all over the sky like an unbroken bronco. His playful hint worked. There were no more flying bridge schools.

The crew was posted to a Lancaster Conversion Unit for a fourteen-day course on Lancasters before joining a squadron and it was here that I had a mortifying come-uppance. A snap examination on the Mark XIV bombsight, fuses and detonators, was held and I returned an almost blank paper. Previous exams had been passed by last minute swotting and something like photographic memory; but the unexpected test revealed the immensity of my ignorance. The chief bombing instructor summoned me and said he couldn't recommend my posting to a squadron. I would be a fatal liability to any crew. In these circumstances there was no alternative but to hold me back and provide the crew with a 'spare bod' bomb-aimer.

I went straight to Dig and told him what had happened. By this time his faith in his crew must have been sorely tried. At Operational Training Unit he had been told that the instructors were making a book on which crew would be the first to get chopped on operations and that his crew were favourites. Paul had disclosed that luck and bluff had carried him through gunnery school; his eyesight really wasn't very good. There was Les's failure in the 'grope' and now I was telling him what the chief bombing instructor had said. He looked anxious at first, but then he grinned. 'The mechanics of a bombsight?' he said. 'I don't give a damn so long as you drop the bombs in the right place.'

He arranged for me to have a special two-day course on the bombsight, fusing, circuits and other technicalities. At the end of the two days I was given a further examination and passed. The crew was then posted to a squadron which had a reputation for moving its base frequently, almost nomadically. Its present temporary base was at Methwold in Norfolk. However, it had been in existence long enough to have its own crest — an hour-glass — and a motto — 'In Time'.

2. *A Debut to Forget*

ON AN AFTERNOON in late September 1944 we walked down a lane which passed a pine plantation. At the end we saw a deserted airfield and for a moment wondered if we were in the right place and had not, by mistake, come to an abandoned camp. Then we understood the reason for the peace and stillness all around. The entire squadron was somewhere over Europe on a daylight operation.

On reporting to the Orderly Room we were given forms which contained questions about next of kin, the disposal of personal articles, and other inquiries that would help the administrative staff to deal with a dead man's belongings, his estate and last wishes. The forms had to be completed as soon as possible.

Dig asked the clerk in charge, 'What's it like here?' He meant, 'Are the billets and food all right?'

The clerk replied, 'It's very good. Haven't lost any since the night three went down over Frankfurt.' He glanced at our uniforms. 'Easy to get commissions too,' he added.

Not only did a subtle status distinction exist between aircrew trades but there was also an open class distinction between commissioned and non-commissioned officers. Paul, who if he hadn't coined the phrase 'I couldn't care less' used it as daily small change, gave a horse laugh and said something about stuffing commissions. Dig who had recently been commissioned but went to extremes to prove that although he was ostensibly an officer and a gentleman he was still one of the boys at heart, felt impelled to make a remark which was sarcastic and at the expense of Orderly Room clerks who gave unsolicited information.

The clerk got his own back. He looked at Dig's navy blue battle-dress, the 'Australia' flash on his shoulders, the winged brevet on his chest, the new ring on his epaulettes, and said, 'It's a funny thing about this squadron. Aussie skippers are very unlucky. We've never had one that's finished a tour.'

Dig said that by Christ he was scared, but it wasn't a good riposte and he knew it. We left the room with the forms and a note of our hut number, and went to the airfield perimeter to await the squadron's return.

It wasn't long before the first Lancaster was sighted, a droning speck in the sky. It was well ahead of the rest and had begun its landing circuit before the others appeared, in ones and twos, in the distance. We watched about sixteen or seventeen land and noticed that two of the aircraft came in on three engines, and we wondered whether the fourth engine of either Lancaster had been knocked out by anti-aircraft fire or had simply failed through some running fault.

By the beginning of October 1944 the Allied drive across France had been halted, the battle-lines had hardened west of the river Meuse, and Bomber Command which had been temporarily tied up with military commitments had resumed a full offensive against large industrial towns in Germany. For two years Sir Arthur Harris (known affectionately to the public as 'Bomber' Harris and less affectionately to aircrews as 'Butcher') had followed a policy of disrupting German industrial, economic and military systems by attacking towns which had a large agglomeration of factories, and saturating these towns by area bombing. Recently, however, there had been pressure on him to be more selective in his targets, and some squadrons, including ours, were being equipped with GH, a new radar blind bombing system.[1]

GH made bomb-aimers with the Mark XIV bombsight almost redundant so that even before beginning operations I belonged to a doomed species which had been bypassed by technological evolution. When using GH the navigator would give a count-down and tell the bomb-aimer when to press the bomb release, and thus the skill of bomb-aiming was reduced to pressing a button which could have been pressed by anybody. However, very few Lancasters were equipped with this wonder gadget and a proficient bomb-aimer was necessary on many raids because GH range was still uncertain. Two yellow bars were painted on the tail fins of aircraft carrying GH equipment and on daylight raids over thick cloud at least two non-GH aircraft would formate on the GH leader and drop their bombs when he dropped his.

It was, of course, by sheer chance that we had joined one of the few GH squadrons in Bomber Command that specialized in daylight target marking.

A battle order was posted on squadron notice boards on Friday, 13th October, and for the first time our names appeared. We retired early to our sleeping quarters, a Nissen hut hidden in a wood some distance from the main camp, knowing that we would be called early.

The call came at two in the morning, and after breakfast Dig, Les and I reported for navigational briefing which was to take place in a large hut filled with trestle tables and collapsible wooden chairs. At one end there was a platform, and the place might have been a village hall, urgently in need of subscriptions for improvements, except for the walls covered with comic cautionary posters. Some of these belonged to the Fougasse 'Famous Last Words' series but one was French and showed a baggy-trousered peasant pulling out the linings of empty pockets. He was standing outside a brothel and the caption ran, '*Avant partir en operations prenez garde que les poches sont vides!*'

Behind the platform a red ribbon, showing the route to and from the target, was pinned to a huge wall-map of Europe. Les settled at a table and began to plot tracks on a Mercator's projection; I did the same on a topographical map. As we worked, a haze of cigarette smoke formed round the electric lights hanging from the ceiling. Dig stood chatting and joking with other pilots and occasionally came across to say, 'How's it going?'

Main briefing, for which pilots, navigators and bomb-aimers were joined by all the other crew members, was opened by the Intelligence Officer. Today's operation against Duisburg was to be, he informed us, the greatest daylight raid ever on a German city. Approximately twelve hundred bomber aircraft would take part in an assault lasting half an hour. Duisburg was only thirty-five miles from the battle-lines and it was the largest river port in Europe. It produced heavy machinery, and its docks and railway marshalling yards were vital communications centres. The attack would be controlled by two Master Bombers code-named 'Bigboy' who would instruct the bomber stream, code-named 'Thunder' as to aiming points over the R/T. The stream would fly at approximately twenty thousand feet and be covered by an umbrella of Spitfires and Mustangs flying at between thirty and thirty-five thousand feet.

The Meteorological Officer then took the stage and predicted that the blanket of cloud which at present extended over England and Northern France would disperse before the stream reached the German border leaving good visibility over the target area. The navigation, bombing, signals and gunnery leaders each spoke a few words and briefing was concluded by the Commanding Officer wishing all crews good luck.

We collected parachutes and, at six in the morning, buses began to transport crews to their aircraft which stood at single dispersal points round the perimeter of the airfield. We travelled in a bus driven by a blonde WAAF who crashed the gears badly. Harry was the only man to speak during the short journey. He said, 'She drives the right vehicle! A truck!'

At the dispersal the rigid bulk of a four-engined bomber stood outlined against the first greyness of dawn.

At one minute past seven Lancaster J-Jig was in position for take-off. Dig opened the throttles wide and the aircraft moved forward, slowly at first because it was carrying 13,000 pounds of bombs, but gradually picking up speed until we were airborne just before the runway's end. Jig quickly entered cloud and for a few minutes we were climbing blind but at eight thousand feet the cloud broke to reveal a brilliantly blue sky. A soft whiteness lay below which spread in every direction to the horizon. There were no other aircraft in sight.

We had been ordered to fly to a point near Ely and to circle for a specified time before setting out for the south coast of England. This time-wasting manoeuvre was to ensure that we arrived at the coast at the same time as bombers coming from northern counties. It was vaguely disconcerting to orbit alone (other locally based bombers should have been circling with us) and I wondered whether Les had made a mistake and we were circling Bristol or Oxford.

Eventually we set course for the coast but as the minutes passed and there were still no other aircraft to be seen Dig checked with Les that we were on the correct course and flying at the briefed airspeed.

On its own J-Jig crossed the invisible English coast and Dig altered course for the French landfall of Abbeville. The sky remained blue and empty and the cloud below was like an endless expanse of snowdrifts.

Dig called on me to take over while he went aft to the Elsan. For a minute or so I flew straight and level on the course given by Les and I wondered, with a sort of nervous pride, how many other bomb-aimers could claim to have flown a Lancaster on operations before dropping a single bomb. Dig came back and I returned to my position in the nose of the aircraft and a perfect view of empty skyscapes above, ahead and below.

George spoke. He had completed transmissions and was fed up with being cooped in the wireless operator's compartment. He said he was going to have a look out of the astrodome. Moments later his microphone clicked on. 'I'm in astrodome,' he said.

'Right, mate,' replied Dig.

There was a brief silence before George spoke again. 'I thought there was supposed to be twelve hundred bastards on this raid,' he said. 'Where's t'other eleven hundred and ninety-nine?'

No one knew the answer.

'One fifty-five was the briefed airspeed, Les?' Dig queried yet again.

'Aye, Dig, but I reckon we're away behind time. We should be over France by now.'

'Increase the revs to twenty-four, Ray,' said Dig. 'Twenty-four,' the flight engineer repeated.

A surge of power ran through J-Jig as it flew towards the blank horizon. The sound of heavy breathing indicated that a microphone had not been switched off. The source of this noise was identifiable a moment later when a tuneless whistle began. Whistling while he worked helped Les to concentrate.

'Microphone, Les,' I said sharply.

There was a click.

The barren blue space ahead seemed more hostile than a sky passage blocked by the feared anvil-shaped cumulonimbus cloud. If the situation hadn't been serious, it would have seemed ludicrous.

21

Here we were, participating in the most massive daylight raid ever mounted against Nazi Germany and we might have been on a solo flight to the North Pole. The squadron motto seemed particularly ironic.

Dig began a steadfast grumble about the other pilots and crews. None of them had followed instructions given at briefing. We had flown according to the book and everyone else had broken the rules. 'It's the last time I ever take any notice of briefed airspeeds,' he said.

It seemed more important to find another aircraft than to bomb the target. For a few minutes no one spoke. Except for the sonorous roar of the engines there was complete silence. My imagination began to wander. We weren't on operations at all. The briefing had been a dream and we were really on a routine training flight. At any moment Les would give the course for base and we should land in time for lunch.

Dig gave a shout. Far ahead and slightly to the right he had seen a couple of specks. J-Jig, with throttles wide open, began to close the gap. Gradually the specks drew closer and were recognizably Lancasters. After a brief discussion with Les, Dig decided to cut a corner and miss Abbeville altogether.

'New course 067,' said Les. 'Swing on now.'

A minute or two later we could see what looked like an attenuated horde of black flies ahead. It wasn't long before Harry made his first comment from the tail. 'Three Lancs behind us,' he said and, in a quieter tone as though speaking to himself, 'In the blasted stream at last.'

Once, for the experience, I had flown in the tail turret of a Wellington, and I knew what Harry must have felt during the last hour. Flying in a tail turret is like being dragged backwards in a goldfish bowl. You sit in frustrated silence while the others speculate about what can be seen ahead, and when at last you see what was being discussed, and can give your opinion, everyone else has lost interest.

A wide rift in the clouds revealed the green fields of France and Harry asked if I could name a town some distance to port which he had glimpsed. As bomb-aimer I was jack of all trades – front gunner, second navigator, understudy pilot and map reader. I said the town must be Dunkirk, still occupied by enemy troops, and Harry seemed gratified by the information. He had come all the way from the West Indies to fly over Europe and now he had seen his first French town.

Far to the left, a vertical vapour trail pierced the sky like a diamond scratch on blue glass. Another V2 bomb had been launched from a German rocket base in Holland.

For half an hour we flew in the security of the stream and then I noticed that aircraft in the distance ahead were wheeling on to a new course. They had bombed and were leaving the target. As Jig flew on, puffs of smoke from flak bursts were visible, tight black balls with a flashing centre that, as they dispersed, became lingering wisps of dark brown. I positioned myself comfortably on my stomach and gave the bombsight and fusing switches a final check. The river Rhine, twenty thousand feet below, was a serpentine thread of silver beyond which spread the dark stain of an extensively built-up city.

Each aircraft seemed to be passing unscathed through the flak bursts and bombs fell like peas shelled from the pods of their undersides. J-Jig lurched slightly as Dig opened the bomb doors. Flak was exploding on either side as through the R/T came the Master Bomber's voice. 'Bigboy One to Thunder, bomb any built-up area. Bigboy One to Thunder, bomb any built-up area.'

To the left, clouds of black smoke were billowing up, but straight ahead, looking like tiny silver tuning-forks, a line of docks was moving rapidly towards the bombsight. There was no time to make any comment — and there would never be a better target — the docks had already reached the intersection of the bombsight graticule, so I pressed the release and said, 'Bombs gone.'

'What?' yelled Dig, who had expected to receive some flying corrections, or at least an indication that I was about to bomb.

The aircraft rose buoyantly as its load was shed.

I heard the camera control click over. 'Bombs gone,' I repeated. 'Jettison bars across. Close bomb doors.'

As the doors closed Dig banked hard to port to follow the rest of the stream.

When we were well clear of anti-aircraft fire I opened the inspection panel to check that the bomb racks were empty and saw with dismay that a 1000-pound bomb was rolling gently around the bomb bay. For some reason this bomb must have been slow to leave its mount and had been trapped by the closing bomb doors before it could fall clear. Had its detonator jarred we should within seconds have become scraps of skin floating in the winds above Duisburg.

I reported that we had a loose bomb rolling around the bottom of the fuselage and told Dig he had better open the bomb doors again.

He said 'Right' and no one else spoke.

Because any movement could have triggered the detonator, it was a bad moment as the doors began to open. But the bomb rolled away and fell in the fashion of all bombs, seeming to drift lazily below the aircraft for a few seconds and then, as it neared the ground, accelerating across the countryside as though in danger of being late for an appointment. I lost sight of it before impact but think it fell in a field and although certain slaughter of many German citizens with the other bombs didn't disturb me (any guilt was collective) I very much hoped that this last bomb (my responsibility) hadn't killed or hurt anyone. But any onlooker in the vicinity watching its descent must have been puzzled why a field had been singled out for one bomb from the disappearing bomber stream. I resolved in future to look through the inspection panel before ordering bomb doors to be closed, and wondered why during training we had been instructed not to make the inspection until well clear of the target.

Back at base, two hours later, the crew was transported to the briefing-room where each man was offered, and readily accepted, a good measure of rum and a few free cigarettes. Dig was our spokesman and replied to most of the Interrogation Officer's questions.

He was asked, 'How about the flak?'

'Not much. Just a bit about.' 'The other crews have reported it as moderate/heavy.'

'Well,' Dig drawled, 'it's our first op, you see.'

'In that case,' said the interrogator in a slightly altered tone, 'congratulations on a successful first operation.' His gaze fell on the 'Jamaica' flash on Harry's sleeve. 'I think *you* deserve a double,' he said, reaching for the bottle of rum.

Nobody mentioned the bomb which had fallen miles from Duisburg.

Paul and I left the briefing room together. We had only walked a few yards when there was a shout. Dig, his hat stuck on the back of his head, and a grin stuck on his face, was hurrying towards us. 'Take it easy,' he said. 'We're on again tonight.'

I felt cheated. Before having any leisure to savour the success of our maiden operation we were being pitched without respite into a second. I complained bitterly.

Dig continued to grin. 'You'd whinge if your arse was on fire,' he said.

Harry joined us. In an imitation of Dig's accent he said, 'I hear we're on again tonight, mate.'

It gave my spirits a slight lift to hear a West Indian attempting to mimic an Australian.

'That's right,' replied Dig.

'Okay,' said Harry in his normal voice, 'but we don't want J-Jig again. That letter's not lucky.'

'What do you mean − not lucky?'

'That Stirling you pranged was a J-Jig.'

Dig looked annoyed. 'We'll fly in what we're given,' he said, and turned abruptly away.

No one slept during the afternoon and after an early supper we reported for briefing. It was a surprise to discover that the target was Duisburg again.

When the navigators had finished plotting tracks and courses, the other crew members were admitted to the briefing room. Harry had time to say, 'It's bloody Jig again,' before silence was called for.

We were assured that the morning's raid had been a tremendous success and that tonight's raid, another thousand-bomber effort, would wipe what was left of Duisburg off the map. The attack would be in two waves and our squadron would be in the van of the first, right behind the Pathfinder Force. To foil the enemy radar system the stream would fly at three thousand feet most of the way across France and then climb to eighteen thousand feet before reaching the battle-lines. Other aircraft would make a diversionary attack on Hamburg and this, with luck, should draw off the enemy night-fighters.

Nobody could remember two separate thousand-bomber raids mounted in such quick succession and for a while there was an atmosphere of excitement, but the sense of occasion was vitiated by inactivity after the briefing, and the high drama of bombing a German city twice within twenty-four hours became the music hall moan of 'Why are we waiting?'

Stranded in a no-man's-land of time, and unable to leave the precincts of the briefing room, it was easy to grow impatient and restless. We smoked and exchanged small talk that was worth nothing more than well-thumbed Monopoly money. Thank God, I thought, that tonight there was to be no orbit over Ely, or a rendezvous with the stream over the south coast. It was a simple matter of flying four legs to the target and four legs back.

The tiny masked light in the bomb-aimer's compartment had to be switched off before take-off but until that time I made myself at home. I felt more secure here than anywhere else in the aircraft. There wasn't sufficient space in which to sit and so I lay, and my couch was the escape hatch. To my left was the bombsight computer box which was connected by two drives to the sighting head which was about eighteen inches away from my nose. The front turret was directly in front of, and above, the sighting head and it contained two Browning .303 machine-guns. To my right, and within reach of my hand, was the pre-selector box on which the order for releasing the bombs could be set and whether they were to fall singly or in salvo. Packed into the remainder of the compartment, and filling all the spare room, were sheaves of 'window' − thin metallized strips of paper which, when fed into the slipstream of hundreds of bombers blurred enemy ground radar screens. It was the bomb-aimer's task to push 'window' through a narrow chute near his right thigh.

While Dig warmed up the engines and tested the magnetos I loaded the front guns and then went aft to stand behind him and Ray for take-off.

It was a dark night and although we had been without sleep for twenty hours nobody felt tired. For me, this was the real thing, a night operation, and excitement at this new experience was stronger than fear for its outcome. The drive to experiment, and the hungry curiosity for adult experience which makes childhood seem in retrospect like a long famine, had not been sated. I didn't realize that vicarious excitement would eventually decline, and that a corresponding line of anxiety would rise, and that at some future point the two would meet on the same level and remain equal for a short while until the line of excitement dipped still further and the anxiety rose more steeply.

Over the English Channel I fused the bombs and put the Brownings on 'Fire'.

J-Jig ploughed through the night and we were encouraged by Les's report that according to his calculations we were making excellent progress and there was not the slightest danger of late arrival. The morning's experience would certainly not be repeated. When next he spoke it was to say that we were so well up on time that we were likely to arrive at the target before the Pathfinders. We were, in fact, leading all the might of a thousand-bomber raid. Eventually, with some anguish, he said, 'We're only two minutes away.'

I peered out at the darkness all around. At this point it was difficult to judge which was more harrowing − to be a long way behind the bomber stream or well ahead of it. I was wondering whether Dig would circle Duisburg and wait for the others to catch up when the night seemed to burst into flower and a rain of red and green blooms fell in front of us.

Les had navigated us to the target dead on time.

Immediately the coloured blooms were sprayed with the deadly sparkle of unleashed flak. It was a spectacle of startling beauty. I dropped our bombs on a cluster of red flares and Dig wheeled the aircraft on to the course for home.

Harry, who had long been silent, said, 'It's not nice to see a guy going down in flames.'

The return journey was routed over the North Sea and before we reached the English coast I climbed into the front turret to unload the guns. I thought they were on 'Safe' and the ammunition belt detached, when I pressed the triggers to clear the bullets in the spouts, but a stream of tracer began snaking ahead and my guns were chattering. At once I released the triggers but Dig thought I had opened fire on an enemy fighter and there was some consternation until I explained what had occurred. 'Bloody good job you didn't shoot down a Lancaster,' he said feelingly.

We landed exactly five hours and twenty minutes after take-off and by the time we had been interrogated, and had breakfast, we were ready for bed.[2]

3. *Home and Faraway*

MY FATHER and mother lived all their married life in an old house at Ganwick Corner, a Green Belt hamlet thirteen miles north of London. I was born in this house and, since my parents had been brought up as Plymouth Brethren, the first years of my life were affected by the narrow doctrines of the so-called Exclusive branch of this sect who believed they were the Lord's Saints and that the world was a Satanic jungle trap. It was the duty of good Brethren to protect their children from worldly decadence — the cinema, radio, professional sport, the Church, public houses, modern novels and dance halls — and although my parents sometimes allowed me to go to the cinema I was sheltered to some extent from 'the World' and sheltered also from the realities which reputedly make or break character — poverty, dominating siblings and emotional insecurity caused by quarrelling parents — and I was shielded, for as long as possible, from knowledge of sex, insanity and violence.

When I was about ten my father broke with the Plymouth Brethren and became a devout Anglo-Catholic. My mother and I followed him to the new church and if Sundays remained drearily sanctified to the worship of God there were few weekday restrictions imposed. Because of our ingrown family life it was natural for me, when learning there was a squadron stand-down, to mount my motor-bike and ride eighty miles to spend the evening at home. Harry travelled with me on the pillion. He was the first coloured man my parents had ever known and they grew very fond of him. His manners were better than those of most of my friends and were accentuated by a charming old-fashioned courtliness. Although he swore as a matter of habit on the squadron he never permitted himself more than 'Good grief!' in my parents' presence, but he used this phrase so often and meaningfully that my mother adopted it as her own.

They didn't entertain much because of food rationing and I think it caused a stir when Harry and I arrived with news of two trips over Germany. I know that from that time whenever she heard a horde of heavy aircraft flying overhead in daylight eastwards towards the Continent my mother would run into the garden waving a white handkerchief she kept ready for that purpose. We never told her that our squadron was unlikely ever to be routed over Ganwick Corner and that she was undoubtedly waving to American Flying Fortresses.

Just as some people experience rheumatic twinges that herald a change in the weather, Harry possessed the gift of knowing when we should be flying. He could forecast with uncanny accuracy from one day to the next whether we should go on operations that day. In addition to being superstitious about aircraft letters, he would never fly unless he was wearing a patterned red and blue scarf.

Dig was superstitious too; he wouldn't fly without his hat, and it had to be placed in a niche behind his head in the cockpit with its peak facing forward. George carried his girl-friend's brassiere as a good luck charm; Paul always wore a yellow scarf patterned with red dragons; but neither Les nor Ray had any faith in charms.

I flew with more tokens than anyone — a silk stocking, a Land Army brooch, a pink chiffon scarf and a tiny bone elephant — and I had a superstitious dread of the third operation for no better reason than that a school friend had been killed on his third operation as a Bomber Command navigator.

When Les and I walked into the briefing room we saw that the target for our third raid was to be Stuttgart. It was to be no sinecure for bomb-aimers. Instead of curling up in our compartments it was obligatory to work the H2S set and plot fixes on a chart. This meant I should have to sit beside Les, blind to the sky outside, and would be in the place where my friend was sitting when he was killed on his third raid.

In my opinion, not shared by anyone in authority, H2S was an overrated device. A scanner under the aircraft's belly sent impulses earthwards and these were refracted back to a small screen when they hit a built-up area. They were manifested as a moving green blob and it was theoretically possible to navigate by H2S alone. One disadvantage was that one had first to find a town, and since the route to Stuttgart had been assiduously planned to avoid all built-up areas it seemed that H2S would have as much value as an unsigned cheque. Another shortcoming was that the scanner gave poor returns if the town was situated in a depression. At briefing crews were informed that Stuttgart lay in the most deceptive of depressions.

We took off in F-Fox late in the afternoon and flew over England in the dusk, but I didn't see the blue-black gradations of nightfall because I was trying to help Les by providing H2S fixes. As it happened, his Gee was operating perfectly and it was he who helped me to find fixes so that my sterile chart could be faked to resemble a genuine navigational record.

As we flew over France Ray began grumbling about having the double duty of 'windowing' and maintaining his engineer's log, and we were both glad when the time arrived for me to go forward to take up a bombing position. Unfortunately, while pushing past him clutching parachute, flimsies and maps, my harness caught on a projection. I wrenched myself free and fell forward into the compartment.

Far to the right, fireglow from the ground showed like a spreading blush on the cloud-tops. I hurriedly plugged in the microphone lead and fastened the oxygen connection. The first words I heard came from Ray. 'You're a stupid twat,' he said. 'Do you know what you've just done? Switched off two petrol cocks!'

I told him that this was entirely his fault; he was far too bloody fat.

Dig ordered us to belt up and then asked, 'Where do we go from here, Mike?'

'See those fires,' I replied. 'Fly over them.'

His question and my answer were both, in a sense, unnecessary. There could be no mistake where the target lay because above the flushed cloud was a flashing barrage of flak. But he was acknowledging the bomb-aimer's right to direct the aircraft over the target area, and I was confirming that I was ready for the run-in.

A few Pathfinder flares floated down and I was too busy giving Dig alignment corrections to notice the flak; it was an urgent matter of unloading the bombs before a selected red flare disappeared into cloud. Once the bombs were clear we headed south for the turning-point at Reutlingen, and west for base. I remained in the nose shelling out 'window's having decided to report the H2S set either unserviceable or totally inadequate.

Half-way home a fault developed in the interior heating system and it became excessively hot in the pilot's cabin and my compartment; then Ray announced that the aircraft's anti-freeze system wasn't working properly and the wings were in danger of icing. Too hot within, and too cold without, it seemed that we were the ingredients of a *bombe surprise*. To get cool I climbed into the front turret but needles of chill air piercing down the gun barrels eventually prodded me back to the over-heated compartment. I must have drowsed into sleep because suddenly Les was saying, 'Can you not see base yet, Dig?'

A few minutes later we landed, the third operation was over, and I need not have worried. For the most part it had been a long and rather tedious flight. Once again I had learned that if one goes through with something one dreads, the experience is never quite as dreadful as one imagines. It is a lesson I am constantly learning afresh and constantly unable to derive any comfort from.

The following evening I telephoned my parents. 'We had some excitement last night,' said my mother, and she told me that a flying bomb had landed only two hundred yards from our house. 'It cracked some windows *and* blew the back door open,' she said.

A new officer arrived to command the squadron. He was a noted disciplinarian who had logged a few minor sorties against the French coast, and his long face was given a look of pre-war conformity by a neat moustache just as a typical suburban semi-detached house of the period was inevitably fronted by a trim privet hedge.

An enclosed stand of dark oak had been installed in the briefing room and from this pulpit he addressed the crews prior to briefing for a daylight raid on Essen. Having spent some years in Training Command he spoke as he had undoubtedly spoken on many occasions to cadets when exhorting them to new heights of keenness, discipline and efficiency, but the main theme of his sermon was to extol the virtues of formation flying. In future the squadron would fly to the target and back in vics of three when operating in daylight, and we would begin these tactics on today's raid. If he had then said he was going to lead the squadron, judgement against him might have been suspended, but he was obliged to fly only once a month on operations and he showed no inclination to embark on this quota or increase it.

As soon as briefing had finished disgruntled crews exchanged opinions about the new man and in a wave of common consent that swept round the briefing room swifter than a malicious slander he was nicknamed 'the Vicar'. The reaction was unfair because although the tactics he preached seemed unworkable on massive thousand-bomber raids – and today's was to be another 'greatest ever' – it was obvious that on smaller GH raids (and we had yet to take part in one of these) formation flying would be essential. But nobody likes to be told what he should do by someone who possesses a purely theoretical knowledge and the briefing session was just another example of the age-old conflict between the idealist and the realist.

However, as instructed, the squadron dutifully flew in vics of three to Germany (the only squadron to do so) but the flak barrage over Essen was so intense that aircraft began to jink all over the place before spilling their bombs. Discipline went to the winds and the squadron straggled back to base in ones and twos. The Vicar must have been disappointed but he was not so foolish as to bring charges against the pilots for having broken formation over the target.

The morning was cloudless and the sea sparkled as we flew towards the Dutch coast, part of a small force sent to destroy German gun emplacements built near West Kapelle on the unsubmerged rim of Walcheren Island. The Lancasters went in low against light anti-aircraft fire. I saw some emplacements lying at the top of a narrow beach and gave Dig corrections until the concrete ramparts were drifting straight and fast towards the bombsight graticule. Eleven 1,000-pound bombs and four 500-pound bombs swung down in a forward curve. For a moment I thought the dark cluster was going to fall short, and curl into the sea, but the bombs cleared the water and seemed to race up the beach before exploding directly on the emplacements.

This was the bomb-aimer's ideal target; a military objective with no danger to civilians and everything staked on a direct hit because anything less would have been a complete waste of time and money. When the bombs exploded I felt the elation of a darts player who has scored a double top to win and the satisfaction of a craftsman who has done a good job well.

Dig swung the aircraft into a 180-degree turn and headed back across the sea. 'My oath, I like this kite,' he said. 'It's the best we've had.' He said that as soon as he had sufficient seniority he was going to bag it for his own. At present it 'belonged' to a crew who were half-way through their tour.

After landing he spent some time talking to the ground crew sergeant in charge of A-Able, a Scotsman called Jock Henderson, and learned that Able had more than fifty operations to her credit. I was glad he had found an aircraft that suited him, and even more pleased when our photographs were developed. These showed that the bombs had fallen accurately; it had been a 'wizard prang'; an alpha for marksmanship.

The next three raids (one at night against Cologne and two in daylight against Solingen) were relatively uneventful except that on the second Solingen trip the Lancasters were bunched so close that at least three were bombed out of the sky by their fellows flying directly above. In addition the defences sent up 'scarecrows', a terror weapon which when it exploded simulated a direct hit on a Lancaster, even to bits of wing descending from a flaming ball of oily black smoke. For a while, the sky above Solingen was an awesome sight.[3]

On the following day during a GH training exercise Dig asked Les to take over the controls while he went to the Elsan. I can't remember why he asked Les to fly, but it was a crazy request. Les had never touched a control column in his life and knew as much about piloting as about the second coming of Christ. When he and Dig changed places his parachute harness fouled the throttles and we began to skate erratically across the sky, but finally he was installed in the pilot's seat and after being assured by Dig that the aircraft was on 'automatic pilot' and a beaut to fly, he was left in charge.

A fore and aft movement was instantly discernible; the aircraft might have been a dinghy gently riding an ocean swell. Harry, whose knowledge of piloting, or parousia for that matter, was on a par with Les's, began to issue agitated instructions from the tail. The motion became increasingly violent and I wondered whether Dig would be able to scramble over the flapjack and main bulkhead on his return journey. It was a tremendous relief to hear his voice on the intercom again and feel the aircraft respond to his sure touch.

After landing I told Dig that we couldn't go through a tour of operations with him having a slash in the back while someone up front tried to hang the kite to a nail in the sky.

Les, who was listening, endorsed this opinion with the conviction of a man who can argue from hard experience. 'I agree with Mike,' he said. 'I was shit-scared when you told me to take over.'

Dig asked us to suggest an alternative.

'Take a pot,' I said.

'I'm not taking a bloody pot...Anyway, who would empty it?'

But he relented, and for the next flight arrived with a large tin that had once contained fruit. He said, 'This is my can,' and from then on this article of utility was known as 'Dig's can' and went everywhere with us. It was my job to empty the can down the 'window' chute after use.

Then we went on leave.[4]

. . . . .

We returned to Norfolk seven days later to discover that, due to fog, the entire squadron had been diverted elsewhere and there would be no flying until the aircraft returned.

The following days had a detached, dream-like quality. A mesh of mist trailed over trees that were bare except for sprays of yellowing leaves and the sweet smell of decaying vegetation prevailed over the more familiar smells of high octane fuel and exhaust fumes. Even time seemed to hover like the mist. Sounds became muted and colours blurred in this soft null of drifting November.

Then a love affair blossomed among the damp huts and dripping trees, and because it was my love affair I cannot write about it objectively. I can only state that the woman with whom I fell in love was a WAAF. There was something fragile and fawn-like about her, even in severe grey uniform. Her name was, and is, Audrey.

We had four evenings together before she was posted to London for a meteorological course. The weather clamp lifted, the squadron returned, and the air was loud once more with the angry sound of engines. Life was almost back to normal.

4. *The Beginning of Fear*

THE TARGET WAS the Kalk marshalling yards in Cologne and we were to fly in Dig's favourite, A-Able. For the take-off I stood behind Ray while he assisted Dig. The procedure was always the same. Dig would turn the aircraft into line with the runway, close his cabin window, say 'Turret to port, Harry', give a thumbs-up signal to the few spectators huddled at the runway's end, advance the throttles with the brakes on, take off the brakes slowly, advance the throttles further as the aircraft surged forward, begin to pedal the rudder controls with both legs, take his right hand off the throttles so that both hands could grip the control column, say 'Okay, Ray, through the gates,' Ray would push the throttles to their furthest extent, Dig would ease back the column, and the aircraft would become airborne. On aircraft where no 'gates' were provided an automatic boost cut-out lever was available to give extra power, and Dig's instructions were then, 'Pull the tittie, Ray.'

During this procedure it was my job to watch the engineer's panel where, among other instruments, there were four small sockets in a row. If the lights in any of these sockets glowed red it meant that the engineer had approximately fifteen seconds in which to switch over the petrol cocks before an engine cut from fuel starvation. To my horror, just as we were about to become airborne a red light came on. I told Ray at once but he was still managing the throttles, and so I continued to stare helplessly at the light wondering whether at any second an engine would cut, A-Able would dip one wing violently, and we should score a terrible furrow across the field below. But in due time Ray turned and, without fuss, attended to the problem of switching tanks.

The anxiety on take-off didn't dissipate during the flight. This was our third sortie since returning from leave and our third raid as a

GH leader. The other two raids hadn't been blueprints for success. Returning from the first, a daylight sortie on Gelsenkirchen, George had suddenly shouted, 'Fishpond's on fire!' We had been hit by flak over the target and this damage must have caused a short circuit in the radar device known as 'Fishpond' in George's compartment. Thick blue smoke, with the acrid stink of burned bakelite drifted into the front compartments and, to prevent us from suffocating, Dig had wrenched open his window. The smoke had billowed out in such density that both our followers, thinking we were about to blow up, had sheered off like startled partridges, never to be seen again. It wasn't an auspicious beginning as a GH leader.

The fire had been eventually put out after a confusion of cross-talk over the intercom. George hadn't been able to find his extinguisher, Les couldn't find his, Ray couldn't find his, and by this time Dig had become quite desperate asking if someone could find a bloody extinguisher. With six cached away on the aircraft he wasn't asking too much. I passed back my extinguisher and George put out the fire, and then immediately found his missing extinguisher. It was hurriedly passed forward to me so that we could pretend that his had been used and not mine.

The following trip had been to Fulda. Harry and I were in London, absent without leave, when he had a hunch that there might be an early morning call. So we set off at midnight and rode back to camp arriving at three in the morning to find that a rush battle-order had been posted and that we were just in time for a pre-briefing meal. As if it wasn't bad enough to go on a raid feeling dog-tired, our fatigue was increased when we learned that the main object of the attack on Fulda, an ancient cathedral town of minor military importance, was to test whether GH operated at a range of nine degrees forty minutes east of Greenwich. This was to be the deepest GH penetration ever and consequently would be a long and tiring journey. When Harry and I finally got to bed at four in the afternoon we were rewarded by the knowledge that GH had proved quite useless over Fulda. Bombs had been unloaded in the hope that they would find their way through cloud to some railway sidings.[5]

And now we were on our third trip with two followers stacked neatly on each side of Able's tail. My uneasiness became acute as we flew towards a fierce flak barrage and a Lancaster ahead went down in a cartwheel of flame. Almost at once A-Able was raked with flak; and again we heard the sound of an explosion followed by the metallic noise of shell fragments raining on to the fuselage. But no vital points had been pierced, and we flew on and dropped our bombs. I was still clutching the bomb release when a delayed wave of shock made my body almost unbearably hot with a prickling heat, and my face felt as though it was being jabbed by a hundred pins.

Gradually the stinging heat disappeared but then my body started to tremble and I couldn't control the shaking of my legs. Any residual dreams of glory faded and forever vanished in the daylight above Cologne. From now on survival dominated my thoughts.

I said nothing of my attack of nerves to the others but hoped it would not be too long before we flew again because the experience seemed comparable to being thrown by a horse, or being involved in a car accident. It was always said that one should remount, or drive another car, as soon as possible.

What worried me most was that if I couldn't recover my nerve I might be grounded with the verdict 'Lack of Moral Fibre' against my name. The spectre of L.M.F. (it was always referred to by initials) had haunted me since training days. One was told of cowards who had been stripped of their rank and put on latrine cleaning duties for the remainder of their service. To go L.M.F. one simply reported to the Medical Officer that the hazards of flying couldn't be faced any longer. Since all aircrew were volunteers, no one could be forced to fly, but the humiliation and ignominy which followed the confession of a stricken man were such that some men continued to fly long after their nerves were in shreds rather than go L.M.F.

While waiting for the next battle-order I recalled the last case of L.M.F. An air gunner we knew on a neighbouring squadron had refused to fly again after seeing a Lancaster blown to bits by a direct hit from flak. He had been stripped of rank and posted away in disgrace. It wasn't so much the admission of fear, and loss of self-respect, that deterred men from going L.M.F., it was the awareness that they would be regarded as inadequate to the pressures of war in a country totally committed to the winning of war. In this atmosphere the man who opted out was a pariah; he was an insult to the national need. He was conscious of bringing shame to his family, and that most of his friends wouldn't wish to recognize him or, at best, they would be embarrassed and awkward on meeting. Nobody cared about the explanations of the psychiatrists – contemptuously dismissed as 'trick cyclists' – and medical knowledge on stress-induced illness was scant.

I had to wait less than twenty-four hours for a battle-order. It was to be a night operation and during the evening crews were briefed for a raid on Neuss. While we and other Lancaster squadrons were bombing Neuss a strong force of Halifaxes would be bombing Essen, some forty miles to the north. The two streams would fly together as far as the battle-lines and then diverge into two prongs.

Take-off was delayed in the hope of an improvement in weather conditions over the Continent and it wasn't until three in the morning that we became airborne. It was a fine night and the cloud below was vividly white. From time to time we saw another bomber flying on the same course and at one point passed over a slowly orbiting Flying Fortress which was manned by a team of wireless operators jamming enemy frequencies.

Eventually we saw a red glow in the distance from the direction of Essen, and flak began to flash around, but we were clear of Neuss before the defences were fully active. Just as we were leaving the target area Dig yanked back the stick and nearly stalled the aircraft to avoid colliding with a stray Halifax which skated by below. This was the only bad moment of the flight and I began to feel ashamed of having felt so frightened over Cologne, and glad I hadn't mentioned it to anyone.

'Next one's Number 12A,' said George as we ate breakfast. No one made any comment and I wondered if the others were beginning to feel the strain.[6]

Rumours of a move had sneaked round the camp for some time and, a week after the Neuss raid, the Vicar announced that the squadron would shortly be moving to a base in Suffolk. It would be necessary to transfer equipment to the new place and for a few days there would be no flying. I decided to slip down to London to see Audrey and arranged a date over the telephone; but I should have

40

known better than to believe there would be no flying. A battle-order was posted for an immediate operation, said to be a rush job and very urgent.

The only rush was in navigational and main briefing which was compressed into about twenty minutes; we were then sent to stamp our feet at the dispersal to await instructions for take-off to Dortmund.

It was a chill morning in early December and swollen clouds huddled in the sky. Harry continuously whistled the opening bars of the overture to *The Barber of Seville*, and I didn't know whether this was to alleviate boredom or to keep up his spirits before the thirteenth operation so I asked why he liked this snatch of music. He said it reminded him of a girl he knew in Kingston who played with the violins in the Edward Gordons orchestra.

'Claire?' I asked. His regular girl-friend was someone called Claire MacFarlane.

'Not Claire,' he said. 'It's a woman I hardly know at all really. Just to say "Hello" to.'

'What's her name?'

'Odalia Marcella O'Raine,' he said.

This captivating name was the only bright moment in a period of vitiating, restless waiting. There was nothing worse than being briefed and then delayed interminably at the dispersal. Every contact with ordinary existence had been severed but no connection had been made with the potential death sequence. Dig and George played football with a stone while the rest of us wandered aimlessly around the concrete apron, sometimes exchanging a remark about the worsening weather, and smoking an endless succession of cigarettes. Harry refused to be drawn into conversation, preferring to stand alone whistling between his teeth.

It was a welcome diversion when a mobile canteen arrived with spam sandwiches and doughnuts.

After almost two hours' delay an immediate take-off was signalled. By now, thoroughly cold and fed up, we climbed into the aircraft.

The trip seemed to last for ever. A brief flak display over the target, and a fruitless search by Dig among the bunched Lancasters for his pal Gog, enlivened the flight temporarily, and then the long crawl home began. In fact, the flight was shorter than most, lasting only four hours and fifteen minutes, but it seemed a foretaste of eternity, a slice of everlasting life.

We touched down at dusk, the last landing at the airfield set in pine plantations, but it wasn't a sentimental occasion and I felt too tired to travel to London.

My own bike was unserviceable so I borrowed Paul's and went to the village to telephone Audrey but when we spoke she seemed so disappointed that I changed my mind about going to London.

Back at the hut I asked Paul for a further loan of his bike. 'Okay, take her,' he said with the air of a man who has suffered everything, including the loan of his girl-friend for the night.

Later, lying in bed with Audrey asleep beside me, I began thinking 'Seventeen to go' with the same compulsive repetition that had obsessed Harry when he had whistled the shrill snatch from an overture by Rossini.

We were detailed to fly A-Able, now recognized as Dig's aircraft, to the new base and our kit was loaded on her, but the motor-bikes had to go by road. Paul's was in a garage being overhauled, which left Dig's Matchless that George agreed to take, and my Norton. George and I arrived before the squadron aircraft and were directed to a Nissen hut which smelled damp and was furnished with nothing more than a dozen iron bedsteads. I claimed a bed near a rusty stove in the centre of the hut.

The Sergeants' Mess was on the far side of a muddy field and we had to wade through water to reach the front door. However, the interior was cheerful; a log fire blazed in a red brick hearth, there were armchairs and magazines, and a baby grand piano stood like a starlet waiting to be discovered on a small stage in the corner. It was in tune and immediately the place was halfway to being home; a piano symbolized friendship, comfort and security, and was to me what a Union Jack was to a patriot, dollar bills to a financier, and bosom to a baby.

The squadron arrived and soon the place swarmed with aircrew. Dig lost no time in telling us what a treat we'd missed. The Vicar had ordered the squadron to formate, circle the airfield once in formation, and then set course for the new base. A recently appointed station commander, a Group Captain, would be watching the display and the Vicar wanted a good show. He was given a good show, said Dig. Instead of formating, the Lancasters came in singly at ground level and showered the Vicar and Group Captain with strips of window and rolls of toilet paper.

I went (absent without leave) to London the following evening and Audrey gave me a blood red scarf to wear for luck. The road was frozen and I skidded many times before the bike slithered in one direction and I went in the other. An Army dispatch rider just missed my head and I scrambled clear before a lorry went straight into the bike.

The lorry driver helped me to haul the immobilized bike into a yard by a butcher's shop and I began to panic. If there was an early morning raid, and our crew was on the battle-order, the punishment would be severe. At the least I would be sent to Sheffield for a discipline course and miss completing the tour with the crew.

It took four hours by hitch-hike, train and taxi to reach base and as the taxi drove past the airfield my anxiety plunged deeper. There was no sign of any aircraft; the squadron must be operating. I went to the hut, but it was empty, and so were the other huts. Fearful and depressed I walked to the briefing room. It was deserted. Then I saw an airman and I asked if there was an operation on. He said that there was. To the inquiry about whether Dig was flying he replied, 'Sorry, haven't a clue.'

I proceeded to the bombing section but already part of me was in Sheffield marching at the double with a full pack. Then I saw a familiar figure leaning against a doorway. For a split second I wondered if I was seeing some sort of glorious mirage. I called, 'Hello, George.'

He didn't vanish. He called back, 'Hiya, Mike,' and smiled.

Surely he wouldn't smile if I was in trouble.

'So we're not on?' I asked.

'No,' he said. 'Bloody nearly were though. We were stand-by crew.'

We chatted for a few moments and then he asked, 'That a new scarf?'

I told him Audrey had given it me for luck.

'You'll need it,' he said with a laugh. 'Dig's furious with you.'

5. *Witten*

AMONG MY POSSESSIONS was a fur-lined leather jacket which had once belonged to a Coastal Command flyer. It had been taken off his drowned body and the zip fastener was ruined by sea water. Because of its morbid associations I wore it only on motor-bike journeys, but when Paul said his electrically heated suit was defective, and he asked if he might borrow the jacket for our next flight, I couldn't refuse. He had often lent me his bike. Nevertheless I didn't like the idea of him wearing a dead man's gear, but I said nothing about its history and he donned the jacket.

Twelve crews assembled for briefing which took place after breakfast and they were told that Witten, a railway town on the River Ruhr, would be a virgin target. It was to be a GH operation with about two hundred Lancasters covered by a fighter escort of Mustangs. Among the crews, and listening eagerly to their first briefing, was a crew led by Flight Lieutenant Harry Warwick. He had flown with us to Ostafeld the previous day to gain operational experience, an exercise known as 'taking a second dickie'. Warwick had been Dig's 'second dickie' and had impressed us with his enthusiasm. He could hardly wait to lead his own crew on an operation, and before leaving the briefing room we wished him and his crew good luck.

A-Able was temporarily unserviceable and we were flying in P-Peter. At precisely 1109 hours Dig eased off the brakes, gave the thumbs-up signal, and began his fifteenth operational take-off.

As we gathered speed I noticed that a gauge on the engineer's panel indicated an excessively high temperature on the starboard inner engine. When Ray had finished take-off duties I asked what this meant.

'It means feathering if we're not careful,' he replied.

45

I scrambled down into the nose and wished I hadn't lent Paul the jacket.

A few minutes later Les came through on the intercom. 'Well, Mike, you come into your own today. Gee's u/s.'

I told him it was impossible to map read. We were above ten-tenths cloud.

Dig came in. 'We'll be right,' he said. 'I can see Easy. We'll follow her.'

The aircraft from our squadron were leading the stream today, and the crew of E-Easy, whose last operation this was, were leading the squadron. For once we were glad of the Vicar's insistence that crews must fly in formation to the target.

E-Easy had two followers and Dig closed in on the starboard side with our two followers. To port, formating with equal exactitude, was Warwick in C-Charlie. He also had two followers.

As the stream spearheaded by E-Easy passed over France Harry expressed satisfaction at seeing so many aircraft behind him. He had never forgotten the loneliness of the first operation.

Ray announced that the starboard inner engine was functioning well and Dig asked for his can. A few moments later it was passed forward and I tipped out its contents watching the urine freeze into smears of ice as it touched the sides of the 'window' chute.

We were about thirty miles from the target when Dig said, 'What do you make of those specks ahead, Mike?'

I climbed into the front turret. In the blue distance it seemed that a cluster of midges were darting erratically up and down; then one fell, leaving a thin spiral of smoke in its wake. 'It looks like a dog-fight,' I said, and the words as they passed my lips sounded strange, an echo of schoolboy magazines and stories of aerial combat.

'My oath,' said Dig. 'Where's our fighter cover?'

Les came out of his compartment to stand behind Ray. 'That's our cover, coping,' he said.

'How the hell does Jerry know about it?' asked Dig. 'This is supposed to be a virgin target.'

'Looks more like a whore to me,' Paul's voice piped through.

As we began the run-in it was clear that ME 109s and FW 190s outnumbered the Mustangs. Flak began to explode and it was remarkably accurate; the ground gunners had estimated the range of the bomber stream precisely from the first shot. Immediately C-Charlie was hit and a stream of oil began to bleed from its port inner engine.

The German fighters, ignoring the risk of being shot down by their own defences, began to mix with the bombers. I glanced below. An ME 109, its white cross looking newly painted on a green and black fuselage, was beginning a curve of pursuit on a Lancaster.

Dig said, 'Bomb doors open,' and I gripped the release.

The ME 109 closed in on the Lancaster which began to swing gently to the left. Its rear gunner opened fire but his tracer went wide of the fighter which returned the fire. Suddenly the rear gunner rotated his turret and fell out backwards; for two or three seconds he rolled over and over in the sky, then he pulled his ripcord and a white parachute blossomed. A burst of flame came from one of the Lancaster's engines, its nose went down, and it spiralled away out of control.

Dig and Harry came on the intercom almost simultaneously. Harry was reporting two Lancasters going down; Dig had seen a Messerschmitt wing falling past.

Les called, 'Make that course 220, Dig.'

'220.'

'Make it 198.'

'198.'

'Make it 190.'

'190.'

'Okay, tittie pressed.'

'Look at that fucking flak!'

'Keep quiet, George,' bawled Dig.

'Another Lanc's had it,' said Paul.

'Flash gone,' said Les. 'Let 'em go, Mike.'

'Bombs going, bombs gone...Jettison's across. Close bomb doors.'

'Closing bomb doors.'

'An alter course coming up, Dig.'

'Don't worry, Les. I'm sticking to these bods.'

Paul said, 'Can we have a banking search, Dig?'

'Get weaving,' George shouted.

I said, 'For Christ's sake stop nattering!'

Dig's angry voice nearly shattered my eardrums. 'Don't *you* start,' he bellowed.

We were in a bunch of eight Lancasters, well ahead of the rest of the stream which was still being mauled by fighters, and the eight constantly weaved among each other like cross-country runners changing places. At one point we were leading the others, a situation which made Harry remark, 'However late we start, we're always in front coming home.'

But it was the only joke he made. He had seen both our followers shot down, but at the vital moment the enemy fighters had been unsighted and he had sat powerless behind his guns.

C-Charlie, oil still pouring from its engine, clung desperately to the leaders, but over France it began to lag and Harry kept up a running commentary on its position. We were glad to hear that a Mustang had found it and was flying protectively close. By the time we reached the French coast C-Charlie was out of sight; Warwick's crew were having a tough journey for their maiden operation, but we had our own problem of descending through thick cloud locating base without the aid of Gee.

When we found the unfamiliar Suffolk airfield (it was our second flight from this base) cloud had descended in a white blight and Dig had difficulty in seeing the runway. Twice he overshot; on the third attempt he was successful.

Of the twelve squadron aircraft that had taken off we were the tenth and last to land.

During the evening, when we were drinking in the Mess, news came through that Warwick's crew in C-Charlie had ditched in the sea and been rescued.

The other missing Lancaster, Q-Queenie, had blown up over the target. There was no hope of any survivors.[7]

6. *The Lost Operations*

EAST ANGLIA was muffled in cloud and the crew played countless rubbers of bridge as rain seeped through the doors and window-frames of the hut. The stove was fed with coke, and draught vents adjusted, so that its heat at close range was unbearable and one had to put on flying gauntlets before toasting a piece of bread. Prudent theft had ensured a full coke bunker, plus an emergency supply under my bed, and we took it in turns to steal bread, butter and jam from the Mess.

The trip to Witten had left an aftermath of uncertainty. The official version of the raid, published in *The Times*, was 'R.A.F. Lancasters escorted by Mustangs of R.A.F. Fighter Command attacked Witten, an industrial and railway town in the Ruhr yesterday afternoon. The Mustangs destroyed six enemy aircraft and damaged others without loss to themselves.' Perhaps it was true; no Mustangs had been lost, but many Lancasters had not returned, and why wasn't this loss mentioned? Stories were still coming in of aircraft belonging to other squadrons which had gone down over the target. The official release was a fine example of information distorted by omission. And why was it that suddenly the Luftwaffe was very active, not merely at Witten but in enormous air battles between hundreds of German fighters and hundreds of U.S.A.A.F. bombers?

Four days after the Witten raid Hitler's counter-offensive in the Ardennes was unleashed and, if the intense aerial activity was not connected with the surprise attack on land, each was independent testimony that Hitler, if he sensed defeat, intended to go down fighting.

The meteorological forecast was of continuing cloud and rain. To lessen the boredom of a protracted stand-by the Sergeants' Mess committee organized a dance. Girls to supplement W.A.A.F.

personnel were ferried in from Bury St Edmunds but even so there was a surplus of males which was increased by one when Dig strolled in wearing a sergeant's uniform borrowed for the occasion. It was strictly forbidden for commissioned officers to enter the Sergeants' Mess except on duty and we all thought Dig's appearance more of a joke than it really was. Even the normally taciturn Warrant Officer Evers came across to ask with a grin whether Dig was keeping an eye on his crew. 'Or should they be keeping an eye on you?' he added.

Among us amateurs Evers was the professional flyer, a pre-war pilot who had logged more than two thousand hours and who, although he had started his operational career later than us, had with a professional's single-mindedness contrived to fly on more operations. He had thirteen remaining against our fifteen. It was while we were talking to Evers that the Vicar, accompanied by the new Group Captain, entered the Mess. They stood by the door, a few feet from us, and gazed at the dancing like benign parents at a children's party.

'What the hell shall I do?' asked Dig in some agitation.

'There's only one entrance and therefore only one exit,' said Evers. 'You need a diversion.'

Paul's thin face became mischievous. 'Watch this,' he said. 'A diversion.'

Clutching a pint of beer he swayed across to the Vicar. 'Hello, sir. Slumming?'

The Vicar regarded him coldly as Paul burbled on. Meanwhile, Dig sloped past the Vicar, head averted, and vanished through the door. But he had not gone undetected. The Vicar swung round and peered after him. 'Good God!' he said. 'That looked like Klenner.'

'Klenner?' said the Group Captain.

'But if it was, he was wearing an NCO's uniform.'

'Extraordinary,' said the Group Captain.

Paul began to edge away. 'Don't leave us, sergeant,' said the Group Captain.

'No, sir?'

'No. I have a question to ask.'

'Sir?'

'Who is your skipper, sergeant?'

Paul feigned intense concentration. At last his frown lightened. 'It's Flying Officer Klenner, sir.'

'I see,' said the Group Captain. 'Let us hope that your future operations are as successful as this one.'

'Yes, sir.'

'Now go.'

The cloud lifted slightly and a battle-order was posted. The Vicar's name headed the list of crews. However, during briefing for a daylight sortie an order was received to cancel the operation. On the next day, with the same crews on the battle-order, a second briefing began, again to be interrupted, again to be cancelled. Less than two hours later the message came to stand-by for a night raid. Armourers were frantically unloading bombs from the bays which indicated that this was to be a long-distance trip with an extra load of fuel. A rumour spread that the Vicar had taken his name off the battle-order, but this was not true. Briefing took place early in the evening and Leipzig was the objective. Perhaps the Vicar had heard of the unkind rumour; he used the pronoun 'we' frequently and with a slight emphasis – '*We* shall be taking-off at 2200 hours.'

Briefing had almost ended when an orderly came running in. 'A telephone call for you, sir.'

The Vicar hurried out. Within a minute he was back. Throwing up his right arm to lead a cheer he cried, 'Scrubbed, chaps!'

Hurrahs of relief and howls of derision blended in the responding cheer.

The crew's second leave began just before Christmas and George, who was getting married, invited the crew to his wedding at Leeds. I was the only one to decline and the reason for what seemed like crew disloyalty was that I wanted to spend every available minute with Audrey who was still on a meteorological course in London.

The daily threat of death had made more acute my love of life, and the temporary reprieve from this threat sharpened an appetite for a life of love. It seemed that all senses were extended and magnified; every waking hour was delightful, every trivial happening of universal significance.

Seven days (perfect except for a skin rash which had developed on my face) passed and on the seventh night Audrey came with me to Liverpool Street station. It was a sad, shadowy terminal, and the lingering odours of engine smoke, damp greatcoats and nameless soups were trapped beneath its grimy roof. Most of the men were in uniform and the women's faces looked strained even when they smiled. We couldn't bear the thought of final waves as my train pulled out; so we kissed and she walked away swiftly. I went up the platform in the opposite direction and by agreement neither looked back.

It was a tedious journey and the train arrived at Bury St Edmunds at two in the morning. I met Ray by chance and we went in search of an hotel, but all the hotels were closed. Rather than walk seven miles to camp we called at the police station and were each given a cell and a couple of blankets. Lying in bed I gazed at bare white walls and vertical iron bars and wondered what it would be like to spend months, or years, in such a place.

The police gave us early morning cups of tea and we cadged a lift on a workmen's bus to camp. Within four minutes of arrival we learned that the crew was on a battle-order for that morning, and that the squadron had lost an aircraft on the previous raid. I didn't feel in tune for flying; moreover, the rash on my face itched badly and would probably be chafed by wearing an oxygen mask.

The scene in the briefing room seemed unfamiliar and strangely fragmented, as though a number of unrelated objects and people had temporarily coalesced in pointless miscellany. Orders were being issued and countermanded, and everyone seemed to have an important message for someone else. I was glad when the briefing was eventually cancelled, not least because Dig and George had not yet returned from leave.

I went to station sick-quarters in search of an ointment and was told that the rash was a form of eczema. My face was painted with gentian violet and I was ordered to stay in hospital. As an up-patient I would rise at five in the morning to help the nursing staff and go to bed at six in the evening.

This was an unexpected and disquieting turn of events. Dig came to see me and I told him I had no idea how long I should remain in hospital but if my face reacted well to treatment I might be discharged within a few days. It wasn't the eczema that worried me, however, it was the rule that if a man missed more than three operations with his crew he became a 'spare bod' and could not complete his tour when his crew completed theirs. Dig listened to my misery and when I'd finished he said, 'It's a great life if you don't weaken,' and left.

On the evening of the second day the whole crew visited me. They had just returned from a raid against a place called Vohwinkel with a spare bomb-aimer. On the run-in he had delayed too long and the aircraft had sailed over the target with bomb doors open but no bombs dropping. 'Sorry, skipper,' he had said. 'Dummy run. Go round again, please.'

At this point in the narrative Harry screwed up his face like a man who has swallowed acid instead of water. 'Can you imagine, man? Go round again!'

Without a word Dig had made a tight circle of the target, all the time under fire, and had begun a second run-in only to find that all the other bombers had gone and he and the crew were receiving the exclusive attention of every anti-aircraft battery within range.

'We told him he'd better get rid of them this time, or else...' said Paul.

'Aye, we told him!' George affirmed with a laugh.

'And he did?' I asked.

'He was too bloody scared not to,' said Dig.

Our crew was not of the stuff of which orbiting Master Bombers were made, and I was secretly pleased that my replacement had been inefficient. Whatever my faults, I had never made a dummy run. So much seemed to have happened since Witten. The others had reconnected with operational flying but for me each new hour of inactivity seemed to slow an impetus that it was desperately important should not be halted. I hadn't brooded about fears felt over Cologne and Witten – presumably some defence mechanism of the mind was repressing unnecessary dreads – but I was becoming apprehensive about the next flight. I was like C-Charlie lagging behind the leaders and unless the gap could be closed I would sink in waters for which no Air Sea Rescue Service existed.

On the last day of the year the Medical Officer gave permission to wash off fading gentian violet and shave. I removed deep purple stubble with a joyous lather and then slunk unobserved from the hospital, mounted my motor-bike and began speeding south.

At Christmas I had promised Audrey we would see in the New Year together. The promise was kept but when, twenty-eight hours after departure, I walked into the hospital ward again I found myself the object of considerable *Schadenfreude*. Not only was a formal charge of Absence without Leave pending, but a police constable had been making inquiries and wanted to interview me. And even worse, the squadron had been operational last night, again against Vohwinkel, and one of our aircraft had been shot down. No one knew the skipper's name but it was certain that he was an Australian.

It was with deep foreboding that I went to see the Medical Officer and, to explain my absence, spun a yarn about domestic troubles. He listened attentively and was not duped. 'I'll see that the charge is withdrawn,' he said, 'but you're not getting away scot-free. You'll stay on here to work. The cookhouse staff is shorthanded.'

I protested. I was quite fit; my face was pure. It was essential not to miss any more operations.

'I'm keeping you on as an up-patient,' he replied firmly. 'It depends on how well you co-operate how quickly you get discharged.'

It was a grim period until I found out that Dig and the others were safe. They were at an aerodrome at Dishforth in Yorkshire having been diverted there with other squadron aircraft due to bad weather conditions over East Anglia. But it was saddening to learn that the bomb-aimer of the crew which had been shot down was George Ingram. George came from a village called Milestone in Saskatchewan and he and I had trained together in Canada. Once on a night bombing exercise over Manitoba he had dropped his practice bombs and, being the worse for drink, gone to the back of the aircraft and fallen asleep. When he awoke he thought that the aircraft had landed and was only just prevented from stepping through the exit three thousand feet above the ground. It seemed that he had been reprieved on that night only to die under an alien sky.

The crew returned from Dishforth in high spirits. Their route to base had taken them over George's home in Yeadon and, before take-off, one of his wife's brassieres had been tied to the tip of one of Harry's guns. Dig had swooped down through factory chimneys, brassiere fluttering gaily, and shot up George's home. The irony was that George's wife had heard the aircraft zoom overhead but had thought that since he was stationed in Suffolk it couldn't possible be his crew, although his younger brother had run out of the house shouting, 'I'll bet it's our George.' George, who had telephoned his wife, began the explanation by saying, 'She thought we were too far away for it to be us,' and was immediately interrupted by Dig, indignant at what he thought was a slur on his pilot's skills. 'I flew down the bloody back passage!' he exclaimed.

The crew went on another daylight raid, the third without me, to Castrop. The Medical Officer summoned me to his office on the following day. After saying that he was discharging me from hospital, fit for all flying duties, he went on, 'You haven't flown for a bit, have you?'

'Three weeks.'

'How do you feel? It'll be rather like starting all over again, won't it?'

'It may. But I don't mind.'

He seemed to be scrutinizing me. 'If ever you're badly worried,' he said, 'I might be able to help.'

I don't know whether he was referring to my spurious 'domestic troubles' or to flying, but it was a friendly offer and for a moment the relationship was not between officer and airman, or doctor and patient, but between two ordinary men caught in a way of life that was natural to neither although both were doing their best to play a convincing part.

'Good-bye then,' he said. 'And good luck.'

'Good-bye, and the same to you.'

For some reason, he looked momentarily disconcerted, then his face quickened to a smile, and I left.

. . . . . .

The hut was empty and my bed, unmade since before Christmas, was a twisted heap of sheets and blankets. It was evident on lifting the blankets that the hoard of fuel had been increased and the bedclothes had been carefully draped to conceal coke. Dirty kit was strewn everywhere. I was back to the reality of squadron life.

Rather than wade through the mire of the field I decided to walk to the Mess by road, but had hardly started when I saw a policeman approaching. He was riding a push bike and slowed down and stepped off as we drew close. 'I'm looking for Flight Sergeant Tripp,' he said.

I felt immediately guilty of whatever crime I might be accused.

'I'm Flight Sergeant Tripp.'

'I thought you might be,' he said. 'Can I see your driving licence and insurance?'

Luckily I had these documents with me in a wallet. I told him about the skid on an icy road and how my bike had been smashed by a lorry. So far as I knew it was still in the butcher's yard. He wrote on a notepad. When the interview was finished he remounted his bicycle.

'What happens next?' I asked.

'That's up to the insurance people, isn't it? I don't think you'll be hearing from us again.'

He cycled off and I continued on my way to the Mess.

The crew seemed pleased to have their regular bomb-aimer back. We sat down to a rubber of bridge. At tea-time a battle-order was posted on the Mess notice board. We were due to fly on the following day.

7. Diversions

THE SQUADRON was briefed to bomb Ludwigshafen, a large industrial town in the Rhine valley. A-Able was again being serviced and the crew had been allocated J-Jig. 'We're always getting Jig,' complained Harry. It was to be our seventh flight in this aircraft.

When I climbed aboard I felt reconnected to the old existence by the stark interior with its trays of ammunition, electrical leads and functional metal brackets, and the peculiar entombed smell of chemical preservatives.

We flew in silence except for the steady roar of engines. Two hours passed and the only talk was when Les gave course and E.T.As. After a prolonged period of quiet Dig shattered the silence. 'This bloody kite's a flying abortion,' he shouted. 'The bastard won't climb.' The stream had been flying at 12,000 feet but as we neared the battle-lines it was necessary to climb to 20,000 feet. Jig made height sluggishly and was still well beneath the stream when Les gave the final course for the target run-in. Lancasters were stacked above and, far higher, there were combats between German and British fighters. In Jig we were like a sardine at the bottom of a packed can.

Black blobs of flak began to appear and it was just as we were entering a well-peppered piece of sky that another Lancaster clipped in front, steadied, slowed, and flew alongside, wing-tip to wing-tip.

'It's young Gog!' bawled Dig.

As dramatically as he had appeared Dig's pal lifted his aircraft away and Paul was saying, 'There's a Lanc. dead above us.'

The flak was now intense and bombs ahead were showering down.

'There's one on top of us!' Paul spoke loudly this time.

'All right, Paul,' acknowledged Dig. 'I'm watching her.'

I glanced through the inspection panel. Jig's bomb doors were open. Les began to count.

There seemed to be more bombs around than flak bursts when he said, 'Now, Mike,' and I pressed the release.

As I turned my head to watch our bombs leave their mounts, J-Jig lurched violently and seemed to fall sideways.

I thought we had been hit and the controls damaged. The sudden change of position at the moment of release made the bombs hesitate on their cradles before rolling down the sides of the doors. I watched them fearfully, but the Cookie lumbered safely away and as suddenly as we had departed from normal flight Dig straightened out J-Jig.

Over the intercom George said, 'Hey, Les, come and see what you just brought us through.' There was a brief silence before George gave a wild cackle of laughter. 'Les is a right lad,' he said. 'He stuck his head in astrodome and ducked down again twice as fast.'

No one else seemed to want to ask the question, so I did. 'What was the point of the fancy flying when we dropped our bombs, mate?'

Dig said that a Lancaster just ahead and above had dropped its bombs so that they fell clear by a few yards, but its Cookie, having less terminal velocity and greater lag than the streamlined 1,000lb bombs, had swung in an arc straight at us. Dig reckoned it had missed us by inches.

The tight concentration of bombers had fanned out on the course for home and Dig and Gog found each other again. The two aircraft flew side by side to England, and there might have been something almost sentimental in the idea of two young Australians, far from home, being united briefly over the target and then flying away together towards the setting sun, but my emotions were untouched. They were flying far too close for safety and my nerves hadn't settled from the shaking over Ludwigshafen. I was glad to land.

After fears on the Cologne raid I had been reassured by an easy night flight to Neuss and curiously this pattern was repeated after Ludwigshafen because on the following night we visited Neuss once more and again it was an uneventful operation.

This left the crew with ten more to fly but before the next battle-order was posted a remarkable piece of news flashed round the camp. George Ingram was alive, the only survivor in his crew, and had hitched-hiked his way back to the squadron travelling all the time with a piece of flak lodged in his back. The Medical Officer was now operating on him in the station hospital.

I went there the next day and after some persuasion was allowed into his room. His face, normally pale and narrow, topped by bristling black hair, was badly scratched and the left eye was bruised and nearly closed. He gave a lop-sided grin and said, 'Hello, there.'

I had recently received a gift parcel of cigarettes from a friend in Canada and I gave George a few packets. He said he was sorry he couldn't offer me anything in return and indicated an opened escape kit on the table. 'I ate the toffee,' he explained. This was no surprise; he had a passion for a certain type of candy bar which cost only five cents and I could remember a conversation during training when someone had turned to him and said, 'What do you think, George?' and he had replied, 'I think I'll go buy a Roxy bar.'

A shirt and battle-dress blouse hung in a corner; the backs of both were torn and heavily discoloured by blood.

It was his habit, he told me, to clip on his parachute over the target area and to remove it when clear, but on this occasion, for no good reason, he left it hanging on the chest clips. The crew were on the return journey and the navigator announced that they were near the battle-lines. For the second time George prepared to unhook the pack and this time actually took it off the clips before fastening it on again. He could give no reason for the impulse; he had never before kept on his parachute for so long, and it still puzzled him why he had behaved differently that night. But he gave no opinions and he didn't mention intuition.

A few seconds after refastening the parachute a burst of flak raked the aircraft from stem to stern and suddenly fire was everywhere. The pilot yelled a single word, and it was his last, 'Jump!'

As bomb-aimer, George was on top of an escape hatch but before he could open it he was thrown hard into the nose against the perspex bowl. He tried to scramble back but the pull of gravity defeated him. His only hope was to burst through the aircraft's nose. He braced his injured back against the perspex and forced with all his might but nothing happened.

He twisted his head to look out and saw snow-covered ground

rushing towards him. 'And by Jesus I tried to break out again,' he said.

He gave a prodigious, frantic heave with back and shoulder muscles and suddenly the aircraft nose broke open and he was falling clear. He pulled the ripcord, was buffeted upwards by violent slipstream, and saw an aerial bonfire score into the snow. A few seconds later he landed on his feet.

He took off his parachute harness, covered it with snow to hide his traces, and began running. He had no idea of direction; he was simply running away from flaming wreckage. When he was too exhausted to go farther he sat down in the snow and looked up at the sky searching for the North Star...'Old Polaris', he said with a laugh...A cross drawn in the snow gave him the cardinal points of the compass and he began walking west. As dawn inched over the horizon a machine-gun opened fire. He dropped flat on his face and lay motionless for a long while. At midday he crawled into a hedge and fell asleep. He awoke to find a small child gazing at him. The child ran off and a few moments later George heard men's voices. Two American soldiers came into view, their rifles trained on him.

He was taken to an advance hospital near Namur but after nearly two days' inactivity, and no proper medical attention, he decided to sell his sidcot flying suit and make his own way back. He bought a meal and hitched a ride to a nearby airport from where a good-natured Dakota pilot gave him a lift to Croydon. From here he went by bus and on foot to Liverpool Street station, and although he had four days' growth of black beard on his face, swollen contusions round his eyes, and a saucer-sized bloodstain round the jagged tear in his battle-dress, his appearance raised no comment. People looked at him, and then looked away. He bought a ticket for Bury St Edmunds at the booking office, and three hours later walked into the Officers' Mess.

I visited him twice more before he was discharged from hospital. A week or so later I saw him sitting alone in the Bombing Section looking miserable. I asked what was the matter. He told me he had just learned that his aircraft had been shot down, not by the Germans, but by an American anti-aircraft unit.

· · · · ·

Most mornings in early January were fine, with cloud spun thinly across the sky, but flying was restricted owing to very bad conditions over the Continent. Each day crews were briefed, drew parachutes, flying rations and escape kits, went to dispersals, and stood around until the signal came that the operation was cancelled. The undischarged tensions of this existence weren't easy to dissipate; men played cards, drank beer, and visited Bury St Edmunds in the hope that there might be a dance at the Corn Exchange.

My motor-bike was still unrepaired and I was beginning to despair of seeing Audrey again when she sent a money order for fifty pounds (her entire savings) with the curt message, 'Get another bike.'

During the period of daily briefing and stand-down I became friendly with a bomb-aimer called Nicky. He had completed one operational tour of thirty operations and, after six months' screening, had started a second. But he was a loner; the rest of his crew were on their first tour, and he had no friends among them. Perhaps it was his air of isolation, a sort of contemptuous insularity, that caught my attention and made me want to know him better. His slicked-back fair hair, his deep-set blue eyes which sometimes seemed to sink behind their own sockets, and his deathly pale complexion prepared me for a man whose emotions were as cold as the frozen expression of wilful detachment on his face.

It wasn't easy to get to know Nicky, and one obtained his acceptance rather like winning the confidence of a wild animal, by frequent contacts and allowing him to sense there was no danger of any sort of aggression until his own aggression was muted to a point where he could accept the suggestion of going together to town for a coffee or a beer.

He was, I suppose, by one definition, completely brutalized. To him, humanity was a degraded species and violent death in action a fitting end to a human animal's life. He was both horrified at the prospect of being killed and yet excited by the idea, and he became alive with a gleeful dread whenever a battle-order was posted.

He seldom laughed unless it was at someone's distress, and the funniest thing he had ever seen was when red danger lights had been removed deliberately from a hole in the road and an unsuspecting motor-cyclist had hit the hole, been thrown, and injured.

As I came to know him better I learned that he had lost touch with his parents and was the father of a three-year-old illegitimate boy. I also discovered that his nerves were in tatters and he was a compulsive risk taker. Sitting on the pillion he would urge me to go as fast as possible, or to overtake on blind corners, and I would accept his 'dares'. And yet the friendship with Nicky provided a sort of equilibrium. I could drink coffee with him, listen to some ruthless illustration of the worst in human nature, and know that I was with someone more scared than myself.

In 1943 he had nearly been killed over Essen and the memory of that raid haunted him. Through some quirk his temperament was utterly opposed to dying on a raid against Essen. To die over Cologne, or Frankfurt, or Nuremberg, would be an acceptable end, but to die over Essen was somehow disgraceful, the ultimate obscenity which he could not stomach.

When, finally, there was no last-minute cancellation, the squadron took off to attack the marshalling yards at Krefeld Uerdingen, and the Group Captain went as a passenger in one of the aircraft. It was to be his first operation. 'Groupie' was popular among aircrews due mainly to a felicitous speech made shortly after arrival. He had then said he intended to remedy the deficiency of being a wingless wonder and to fly operationally because he thought that the station commander should share the same dangers as his men. What made the speech peculiarly attractive was his use of the term 'wingless wonder' which normally denoted an R.A.F. ground staff officer who had not trained as a pilot or for any aircrew trade. In fact, the Group Captain wore pilot's wings on his tunic; he had many flying hours to his credit but since none of these had been operational hours it was a nicely deferential touch, and extremely shrewd, to allude to himself as wingless. Everyone hoped that his first raid would be a success.

Cloud hung in layers almost up to twenty thousand feet but above the topmost layer the Lancasters' wing-tips cut long plumes of vapour against a pure blue sky and created something like an aerial work of art. Even Dig conceded that there was beauty in white contrails lingering against fathomless blue, but he was in a good mood that day, anyway, since he was flying his favourite, A-Able.

Near Krefeld, cloud reached up like a mailed fist and we flew blindly to the target, homing on GH, and uncomfortably aware that two hundred other Lancasters were in the vicinity, all unseen, and all dropping bombs.

Les said, 'Let 'em go,' and our bombs disappeared into a grey-white blanket. The camera began to tick, taking a picture of nothing nowhere, and then Dig closed bomb doors and altered course.

The cloud had thinned slightly and we were flying through rent gauze when I noticed a flak burst directly below. A second later there was a second burst, again directly below, but closer than the first. An anti-aircraft battery had singled us out from the stream and was predicting our course on radar. I shouted to Dig to weave and he put Able into a fierce corkscrew.

Ray muttered, 'Blimey, that was close,' and Dig's voice came through, anxious in tone, 'Are you all right, Les?'

There was no reply.

'Les! Are you all right?' As he spoke, Dig straightened out Able.

'Aye, I'm all right. What's the panic?'

'Bloody great lump of flak through the windscreen right between Ray and me.'

Les drew back the blanket which shielded his compartment from the pilot's cabin and peered through; his eyes seemed to be grinning above his oxygen mask. 'Missed you both?' he said. 'That was a rotten shot!'

'It's torn my bloody sleeve,' replied Ray peevishly. The left sleeve of his battle-dress blouse was ripped between shoulder and elbow.

I laughed aloud.

'Back in your hole, rat,' he said, giving me a push with his boot.

On the way home there was a search for the piece of flak which had caused the damage but strangely it was never found. The hole in the windscreen was stuffed with rags and Dig had to contort himself to look through clear perspex when landing.

Back again for interrogation we saw that the Group Captain had returned safely and was laughing and joking like a veteran. This was the best time of all, when something like euphoria seemed to possess everyone, and it wasn't difficult to imagine that each elated flyer had taken some stimulant drug. Even Nicky smiled and seemed at peace with the world.

Crews were briefed to bomb Saarbrücken and then told to warm up engines and wait at dispersals for further orders, but the cloud was so low that the end of the runway couldn't be seen, and no one expected to fly.

Jock Henderson, Able's ground crew sergeant, had repaired the windscreen by himself, having given the rest of the ground crew a night off, but had fallen off his ladder three times while working single-handed and had rather regretted his generosity. He stood behind Dig and Ray as the engines were warmed and tested. When the oil was circulating freely Dig cut the engines.

For a while the crew strolled round the dispersal stamping their feet and smoking, full of the usual pre-flight disquiet which shows itself in loud laughter and sudden silences. Out of the lightly falling snow the Vicar's car appeared. 'Take-off delayed an hour, chaps. Stand by and if there are no further orders taxi out.'

Another hour to waste. The hedge near Able's dispersal was a pale grey blur; we seemed to be existing in a roll of poorly developed film taken by an unfocused camera. Operations had been cancelled in much better weather and it seemed certain that the marshalling yards at Saarbrücken, jammed with supplies for the German Army, would be spared for another day. I hoped they would; that evening Audrey was coming up to Bury St Edmunds for the week-end, and this was far more important than the dislocation of the already disorganized German transport system.

The hour passed and we took off on a skating rink runway. Dig flew a straight course at a prescribed airspeed to avoid collision and at 9,000 feet the cloud broke into deceptive sunlight with strands of cirrus hanging like paper streamers.

Over the Continent the sky became clear, and, as we approached the target, Saarbrücken looked like a huge cat curled up in the sun. I was reminded of the opening lines of Wordsworth's most famous sonnet as, out of the beauty of the morning, bombs fell and shockwaves shimmered up like a heat haze. As explosion followed explosion the city vanished behind a pall of oily smoke.

Ray said, 'We've got to feather the port outer,' and the journey home started on three engines.

Harry, whose turret was powered by a hydraulic pump operated by the port outer engine, could now only move the turret slowly by manual control and it must have been a comfort to him when a friendly Mustang pilot, observing we were in some difficulty, and on our own, came alongside as escort while a battle between British and German fighters was making long white scratches on the blue sky overhead.

Over the French coast cloud began to form below and I thought of Audrey arriving in Bury at about this time.

George spoke. 'Diversion just come through on the wireless, Dig. To St Eval, wherever the hell that is.'

There was a pause while Les scrambled among his maps and flimsies. 'It's on the Cornish coast,' he said. 'Alter course to 275 till I get a fix.'

We sighted the Cornish coastline at dusk, and at least forty Lancasters were milling around like vultures over a corpse. As we flew over St Eval we saw that the runway had to be approached from the sea. In the poor visibility and deceptive light Dig would have to take care to avoid flying too low and hitting the cliffs. We orbited for a long time before, 'Beany Able prepare to land' came over the R/T.

Dig and Ray went through the drill of lowering undercarriage and flaps but as we turned towards the runway I noticed another Lancaster ahead which seemed far too close.

'Beany Able, funnels,' Dig called to Control, but there was no acknowledgement. '2850 and thirty degrees flap,' he ordered Ray. We continued to close in on the aircraft in front. It was going to be an extremely risky landing.

Then Control came through with a rush. 'Beany Able overshoot, Beany Able overshoot.'

'Beany Able overshooting,' twanged Dig, and he sounded very fed up.

'The engines are pretty warm, better land this time,' said Ray.

Standing behind Dig and Ray in my normal position for landing I could see Able's three engines glowing red, and the fourth a dark silhouette pronged by a rigid propeller. Dusk had ripened to night. Les switched out the lights in his compartment, drew back the blanket, and squashed in behind me. Four watchful faces peered ahead as the landing drill began again. As Able lost height the cliffs racing towards us were barely discernible.

'Beany Able funnels,' said Dig.

'Overshoot Beany Able, overshoot Beany Able,' was the unflurried reply from Control.

'What the hell are you playing at?' snarled Dig. 'Okay, Beany Able overshooting...Full throttle, flaps and wheels up.'

'The engines won't stand much more,' said Ray quietly, 'and we're well into the petrol reserve.'

George left his wireless set and huddled behind Les. Five men were now peering ahead with occasional glances at the glowing engines and the sparks showering into the slipstream.

I had forgotten about Audrey, neglected in a hotel in Bury St Edmunds; the only thing that mattered was to land safely.

For the third time Dig pressed the R/T button and he spoke slowly and distinctly. 'Beany Able funnels. We are on three engines and *must* land.'

'Pancake Able.'

'Able pancaking,' said Dig with relief.

The engines took the strain of full power and we sank over the cliff-tops. Then from nowhere a Lancaster slipped in from starboard just ahead of us; its wheels were down and the pilot obviously intended to land. There wasn't room for both of us and Dig took the only action possible. He called Control and said, 'There is an aircraft ahead of me, Able is overshooting again.'

Able's frame shuddered as for the third time she began to climb on overtaxed engines, and it is at times like this that inanimate matter ceases to be 'it' and becomes 'she'. We were not seven men in a well-constructed metal vehicle but seven men within an object of such overpowering symbolic significance that its components and fuel systems seemed to become flesh and blood.

'Able's never let us down yet,' I said.

'And she never will,' replied Dig.

He made a tight circuit and told Control, 'Get all aircraft out of the way. Able lands this time regardless.'

There was a pause before a clear voice came through. 'All aircraft clear the approach, all aircraft clear the approach. Beany Able go ahead.'

We cheered as Able's wheels touched and held the ground.

After a meal George and I went in search of a telephone. He rang his wife and came out of the booth saying, 'That was wizard!' I wasn't so lucky. Audrey hadn't booked in at the hotel and I didn't know where she was or how to get in touch with her.

George and I returned to the Mess but the others had gone. After a drink with Warrant Officer Evers we searched and found they had taken the last five available beds on the camp. So we wandered towards the camp area reserved for permanent staff and found a room that was reserved for the orderly sergeant's use. It possessed two beds and that was all we needed.

On the next day we flew to base as passengers in another aircraft having learned that Able would be unserviceable for some time.

I was walking through the camp, shortly after landing, when an airman came towards me with his eyes riveted to my red scarf. 'You're Tripp, aren't you?' he asked. He then told me he had met a girl on the previous evening and she had seemed worried about me. She had asked him to look out for me and to give me a telephone number. She had said I would be wearing a red scarf.

A few minutes later I was speaking to Audrey on the telephone. Hers had been a typical experience of the woman who waits. After meeting the airman who had given me the message she had met another airman from the camp who had told her that the squadron had been diverted to Cornwall but that our crew had been posted as missing.

Without washing, or shaving, or changing my clothes, I jumped on the motor-bike purchased with her money and twenty minutes later we were reunited in the genteel lounge of the Angel Hotel. We said 'Hello' and walked straight out of the lounge and upstairs.

8. *The Fault of the English Weather*

NOBODY HAD HEARD of Erkenschwick, not even, apparently, the publishers of the topographical maps we used, but Warrant Officer Evers was given cause to remember it. A piece of flak came through his windscreen. It ripped open his helmet and sliced the top off his right ear. But the accident didn't incapacitate him; that evening he was in the Mess with bandage and sticking plaster over the right side of his head. He and his crew were so keen to finish their tour that they had forgone their leave, and while we still had seven left after the Erkenschwick raid, they had only one. But they were not listed for the raid on the following night and it was rumoured that the Vicar wanted to give them an easy trip to conclude their tour.[8]

Half an hour before midnight we took-off in an almost new Lancaster to bomb an oil plant at Wanne-Eickel in the Ruhr valley. From the start it was a disastrous trip. Dig's side window wouldn't close properly, and he and Ray were obliged to sit in an icy draught. In addition, Ray was suffering from attacks of diarrhoea.

Over France Dig couldn't get the aircraft into 'M' gear (supercharger gear) at 13,000 feet. He was still cursing the gear when Ray was compelled to rush back to the Elsan and it was while he was blundering in the darkness half-way down the fuselage that Paul came through on the intercom to report that the starboard inner engine was on fire. Ray reached the Elsan, plugged in the intercom, heard a babble of talk about an engine being on fire, evacuated himself, and began to struggle back to the front still hauling up his trousers.

The engine wasn't on fire but it was throwing out showers of sparks and gusts of flame. The aircraft vibrated and Dig said that 13,000 feet was its ceiling; he couldn't drag it higher.

The labouring engine was now producing swathes of sparks and

68

flames and Ray decided it must be feathered. Within seconds the engine was dead and we flew on towards Wanne-Eickel on three engines.

Dig asked, 'How are we doing, Les?' and was told that we were about one hundred and sixty miles from the target and already twenty minutes behind schedule.

'We'd have made it in Able,' said Dig, 'but I can't get this bastard to climb. We're going home. Give me a course for the North Sea jettison area.'

This was a dead region of the sea, avoided by all shipping, where, in emergency, bombers could reduce their weight by unloading bombs. By coincidence, the area had been the subject of some discussion the previous week because a navigator had gone L.M.F. after take-off and refused to give his pilot courses for the target. In the end the pilot had flown to the jettison area, unloaded a few bombs, and returned to base. The navigator, a pilot officer, was now awaiting a posting away from the squadron and in the meanwhile could be seen occasionally wandering around on his own, an expression of fixed embarrassment on his face.[9]

Having been unable to climb above 13,000 feet on four engines, Dig now had to plough back across France taking care not to sink below 10,000 feet on three engines because there were American batteries, known as 'Z' batteries, at various points which opened fire on any aircraft flying below 10,000 feet. It was two in the morning and everyone was feeling cold, strained and tired.   It seemed an eternity, with Dig constantly complaining that the remaining engines weren't doing their work, before we reached the French coast. Then Harry, who hated flying over the sea at the best of times, began to complain of the intense cold, and I carped about the fact that this would not be credited as an operation since we hadn't reached the target. Before we took-off there were seven to go and when we landed there would still be seven to go.

Ray began to calculate what bombs should be dropped so that we could land with a safe all-up weight. At length he told me to drop the Cookie and the 500-pound bomb to the rear of it.

I selected the two bombs and we flew on through the night. After about twenty minutes Les said, 'You can drop 'em any time you like, Mike.'

Dig opened the bomb doors and a light blinked by the 'Single and Salvo' bar of the distributor box. I looked into the bowl of blackness below and squeezed the release. The light winked off and the aircraft lifted. 'Don't close the doors yet,' I said to Dig. 'I'll just check.'

I swept a torch beam down the rows of bombs and realized with a sick dismay that I had selected the wrong 500-pound bomb; I had dropped the bomb at one side of the Cookie and not to the rear of it and consequently the aircraft wasn't balanced laterally. I explained what had happened and asked if I should drop the bomb on the other side of the Cookie to redress the balance.

'You are a bright bastard,' Ray exploded.

'Do you want another one off or don't you?'

'Yes, but drop the right one this time.'

I checked my flimsy and set the pre-selector, and the vision of dropping a sequence of wrong bombs swept like a horror film through my mind. I checked again; the setting seemed correct. I closed my eyes and pressed.

The torch revealed three empty bomb positions neatly balanced. I told Dig to close the doors.

Much later Dig made a perfect landing at base.

'As your chief critic,' Harry said to him, 'and since I am the one who gets his head bumped if you make a bad landing, permit me to tell you that your three engine landings are always the best.'

'That's because he has to keep finger out,' said George.

We were a bare half-hour ahead of the men who had successfully raided Wanne-Eickel and ate our breakfast in an atmosphere of pensive gloom. The meal was nearly finished when Harry said, 'I'm glad we didn't press on. As soon as we got airborne I had a feeling there were seven dead men flying.'

There was an uneasy silence.

'Why don't you tell us these things?' said Paul.

Harry went to the Medical Officer and was treated for frostbite on his face and two fingers. His coffee-coloured face was marked with two matching patches of darker brown on each cheekbone, and it was fortunate that the weather clamped so hard for a fortnight that we couldn't fly and his face was given a chance to heal.

Almost daily, however, there were briefings with subsequent cancellations, and on some mornings I went to Bury with Nicky for a coffee and some evenings Harry and I went out to a pub or a dance. Then Nicky went on leave.

The Norton had been moved from the butcher's yard to a garage, but A-Able still languished in Cornwall.

Evers and his crew fretted to fly on their last operation.

Audrey was posted to Mildenhall in Suffolk which was the base for another Three Group squadron.

The cumulative effect of three months of operational life was beginning to tell; tempers were becoming short, and mutual insults were intended to wound rather than amuse. Off duty, Harry and I were seeing less of the others; familiarity hadn't bred contempt, but it had infiltrated boredom.

Dig had given up pretending that he was still a sergeant at heart and we saw less of him. Perhaps he was getting tired of our complaints about the billet, the food, and the Vicar's attempts to instil camp discipline. The phrase 'You'd whinge if your arse was on fire' was never far from his lips and one day when he used it in a quite irrelevant context I explained with ponderous logic, which hid the furious irritation I felt, that there is one time when it is absolutely excusable for a man to whinge and that is precisely when his arse *is* on fire. Dig was not deterred. He continued to use the phrase on improbable pretexts and would then add, with a sidelong glance at me, 'But that, they tell me, is the time to whinge.'

George developed the habit of addressing everyone as 'Kiddie' and whereas he had once been phlegmatic his moods began to fluctuate between facetiousness and despondency. Ray and I could barely speak to each other without quarrelling, and both Les and Paul increased their daily consumption of alcohol.

Audrey came to the Angel Hotel for a night and before going to bed I telephoned Les. In a prearranged code he let me know I must be back at camp by three in the morning. The hotel porter woke me, and Audrey watched as I dressed, shivering in the unheated room.

Back at camp I had breakfast and walked to the briefing room with Nicky. He had enjoyed seven days' leave with a widow who ran a tobacconist's shop. 'She'd let me sleep all day and booze all night and then put me to bed without the usual bloody binding and I'd sleep all next day.'

I asked what he thought the target would be today.

'It should be short and easy,' he said. 'Evers is down for his last and the Vicar is flying.'

The target was the Gremberg marshalling yard at Cologne.

'I can't understand them giving Cologne to Evers,' I said to Paul.

'Haven't you heard?' he replied. 'There was a change of target. When Evers's name went on the battle-order it wasn't Cologne.'

At briefing the Vicar was obviously excited; it would be unfair to say he was jumpy. Our squadron, he said, had been given the honour of leading the stream and Warrant Officer Evers would lead the squadron. 'I'm sure we all wish him and his crew the best of luck,' he added. There was a cheer and a few handclaps. Evers, his ear still covered with a strip of plaster, kept his head lowered.

I was afraid before the trip began. The memory of our previous trip to Cologne had made the city an evil beast just as Nicky's *bête noire* was Essen. As we neared Germany I lay in a funk in my compartment.

The ruined city could be seen on the far side of the Rhine and, before the stream reached it, a formidable warning barrage of flak was pumped up. I found myself throwing out 'window' − a futile occupation in perfect visibility. About a hundred yards ahead there was an explosion, either a Lancaster had been hit or a scarecrow had been thrown up. I heard flak bursts close by and the sound of fragments hitting the fuselage. Harry yelled, 'Get weaving,' and Dig swung the controls so that we wheeled over the sky like a winged bird. The orange graticule was racing up and down the grey streets of Cologne when I let the bombs go. The defences were now flooding the sky with flak and a Lancaster ahead dropped thousands of feet like a stone.

Once clear of the target Paul inspected the fuselage. Our aircraft had been holed in many places between his turret and the tail.

After landing we soon discovered that the customary elation after a successful mission was absent today. Aircraft were limping home and almost everyone had been hit. Nicky's crew came in on three engines, and the Vicar's aircraft had been damaged by a piece of flak which had passed right through the throttle box, missing him by inches. Two squadron crews had been lost over the target. No one mourned the loss of a fairly new crew, but everyone agreed that it was a shame that Evers and his men should get the chop on their last mission.[10]

On the following day, after bombing the marshalling yards at Krefeld Uerdingen, the Vicar came across to Dig. 'I'd like to see you for a few moments,' he said.

Looking perplexed, Dig followed him from the interrogation room. We hung about trying to conjecture why Dig had been singled out. When he returned, his eyes were angry. 'Listen to this,' he said. 'An order came through today that any crew which hadn't completed twenty-five ops by this morning will have to fly an extra five before being tour-expired. That means us. We did our twenty-fifth a few hours too late.'

Instead of five to go, there were now ten.

'If Wanne-Eickel hadn't been abortive, we'd have made it,' said Les.

'That's your bloody English weather for you,' said Dig with what seemed astounding irrelevance.

'We'll never get through another ten,' said George miserably.

'Just our bloody luck,' said Ray.

'It's the weather,' said Dig. 'The weather has bottle-necked the OTU's and there aren't enough crews coming through to replace the tour-expired types.'

This information was greeted by a self-comforting surge of familiar oaths.

'There seem to be a number of arses on fire,' commented Harry dryly.

'Bash in for some leave,' Paul suggested.

'Not a bad idea,' said Dig. He swung round and went straight back to the Vicar. He was back again almost at once. 'We've got it,' he said. 'Seven days' leave and it's immediate.'

Advance Russian troops were now only ninety-five miles from Berlin, but we didn't care.

Audrey timed her leave to coincide with mine and we spent the last part of it in Bury St Edmunds. I arrived back at camp just before midnight on the last day to find that a dawn operation was scheduled.

Breakfast was at two in the morning and then came a long delay. Rain beat against the roof of the briefing room like the scuttering feet of mice and we played cards. We had still not been briefed when daylight began to seep into the sky and it came as no surprise when the hovering Vicar received a message and called, 'Scrubbed, chaps.'

I rode back to Bury while the others returned to the hut for some sleep. I ran up the hotel stairs and into our room. Audrey sat up in bed. 'You're drenched,' she said.

I said I'd like to change my socks and asked if she had a pair.

'Only a pair of stockings.'

She laughed as I rolled on a pair of grey lisle stockings.

We went to a café for a cup of coffee and then wandered round the town looking in shop windows.

I was used to receiving curious glances from civilians, as though I were a missing evolutionary link; my hair hadn't been cut for months and I never wore the standard forage cap; my dress was a mixture of flying gear and ordinary uniform topped by the red scarf; but when a whole crew, wearing their best blue, stopped and stared, I knew I must be looking more than usually Neanderthal. I glanced down and saw two lengths W.A.A.F. stocking trailing the pavement behind my shoes. It is mortifying for an arrogant rule-breaker to be obliged in public to pull up women's stockings under the amused gaze of his fellows. Audrey nearly wept with laughter as I stooped and began to pull up my trouser legs.

Having exhausted the delights of Bury St Edmunds we returned to the hotel. As we walked up the steps I wondered if there would be a message from Les and I went straight to the receptionist's desk. Before I could speak she handed me a note. It said, 'Flight Sergeant Tripp is to return to camp immediately.'

We went silently to our room. I picked up the wet discarded socks and pushed them into a pocket. I told Audrey I would let her have the stockings back when we met again. Today I should be wearing them for luck.

She nodded. Nobody who had seen her in the street a few minutes before would have thought she was the same woman. Her face expressed a containment so set and serious that it could never have been liberated by the sight of her man, fearful of being mistaken for a transvestite, desperately concealing his shame. All fun had vanished. It was a cold wet day, we were about to be parted, and we didn't know when or where or if we should meet again.

'No need to panic,' said Les, as soon as I arrived, 'briefing isn't till eight tonight, but Vicar wants us to get to bed this afternoon for some shut-eye.'

I lay between damp sheets but no sleep came.

As we tramped through fading light to the Mess someone called out, 'Briefing's been put back an hour. Nine o'clock now.'

After a meal George pulled out a pack of cards. 'Penny a hundred,' he said and sat opposite Les. Harry partnered me.

We had been playing for about two hours when an airman began to chalk on the blackboard by the door. He wrote, 'Briefing postponed until 2400 hours, midnight.'

Shortly after, a telephone message came through that all crews were advised to go to bed and expect an early call.

We went to the hut and partially undressed. Audrey's stockings were good for some ribald jests before Ray switched off the lights.

The hut door crashed open, the lights blazed on and a voice shouted, 'Wakey, wakey,' with the sadistic joy of one who is authorized to create disturbance. 'It's twenty past twelve,' said the voice, 'and briefing's at one.'

The door slammed shut. Paul snored.

We had suffered from violent intrusion, why shouldn't Paul suffer too? Les moved to the head and George to the foot of his bed. One, two, three...Up!

'Whathebloodyell,' came a cry from blankets writhing on the floor.

'We're on in ten minutes,' said Les.

Paul's head projected from the pile of bedclothes and his hair stood erect like a coxcomb. 'Get stuffed!' he said.

On arrival at the briefing room we learned that the target was Hohenbudberg, a town on the railway between Duisburg and Krefeld, and the objective was to destroy rolling stock and block the lines which led to Cleve, the point where the Siegfried Line ended. The Intelligence Officer informed us that persistent attacks on marshalling yards and rail communications had almost immobilized the German Army. Transport conditions in the Third Reich were chaotic. A hopelessly disorganized Germany lay between the steel grip of Allied troops on the west and a crushing tidal wave of Russian troops to the east.[11]

We didn't care about the grand design to smash the enemy; all that concerned us was to fly ten more operations and return safely from the tenth.

Take-off time was deferred from two-fifteen to three. We smoked cigarettes and exchanged the smallest talk. Take-off was delayed a further half-hour, but by this time we were so inured to frustration that when we took-off at 03.45 hours it seemed almost as though we had no business to be flying.

The trip was fairly uneventful and after breakfast I went to bed, but before lying down I pulled off Audrey's stockings and rolled them into a woolly ball.

At some time during the afternoon Dig came into the hut and roused us. When everyone was fully awake he sat on the side of a bed, lighted a cigarette, and began, 'You're not going to like this.'

No one spoke.

'Another directive came through from Group today. That order about extending a tour to thirty-five ops has been amended. The order is now "forty sorties over enemy or enemy-occupied territory." '

George broke the dreadful silence. 'But that'll leave us with fourteen to do! We're back where we were two months ago!'

'That's right, mate.'

'We shan't make it,' said George. He spoke with a convinced despair that touched a response in each of us.

9. *The Bombing of Dresden*

WHILE THE OTHERS went to the Mess to see if the bar was open, I went in search of Nicky. 'Haven't you heard,' said one of his crew, and then explained that Nicky was no longer flying with them. On an open night in the Mess and in the presence of a number of lady guests he had said, 'I'll give you something to talk about,' opened his fly-buttons and urinated on the floor. The following day he was sent to Sheffield for a three-week discipline course.[12]

Nicky wasn't normally an exhibitionist and it was a stupid performance; he must have been very drunk and more than usually misanthropic. How far will a man go in an attempt to alienate himself and demonstrate his contempt for ordinary standards of behaviour? Nicky had gone far. But it was a different sort of public leakage which caused the Vicar to summon all crews to the briefing room. Recently, top secret information on targets had been circulating among ground staff, and even civilians, before the crews themselves knew which target they were to bomb. It was suspected that someone on our squadron was responsible for these dangerous revelations and the Vicar asked crews to report immediately anything which seemed suspicious. 'Careless talk costs lives,' he said, 'and I don't have to tell you whose lives are at stake if the German High Command knows in advance where the bomber stream is headed.'

After the meeting had dispersed Dig called the crew together but he had deliberately avoided asking Harry to join us. His reason for this soon became clear.

'We all know what a bloody fine chap Harry is,' he began, and he finished, 'but I can't bloody well understand how he always seems to know when we're going to fly. And he can sometimes make a good guess at the target before we know it.'

Dig's lean jaw seemed to hang uncomfortably on his face as he

77

spoke, and when he stopped talking there was an uncomfortable hiatus which I filled by asking if he believed in intuition.

'Up to a point,' he replied, 'but not every time. And if it is intuition we should warn him to be extra careful not to spill his hunches.'

I agreed, but said this would need considerable tact.

There was another uneasy silence and Dig looked at each of us in turn as though seeking advice. He obviously detested what he felt to be his duty.

In the silence I recalled a peculiar incident which I had never mentioned to the others, and neither had Harry. It had occurred not long after we joined the squadron and before we were a GH trained crew. One morning, half-way through a briefing on a raid against Cologne, the Vicar had announced that a signal had come through which meant a slight delay. We were dismissed from the briefing but instructed to remain in the vicinity.

It had been one of those rare mornings in November when the sky is completely blue and there is a false warmth in the air as though spring has managed to bypass winter. Harry and I strolled through a small pine wood near the briefing room, kicking sticks and cones with our flying-boots. Without any preamble he said, 'Last night I dreamed I was standing by the tombstone of an old friend. Someone who had been killed in an aircrash when I was in Canada. I hadn't been there long before he appeared. He held out his hand to greet me...I don't like that sort of a dream.' If he didn't like it, I hated it.

'But I don't think we shall be flying today,' he said.

With this small consolation we wandered back towards the briefing room, and although Harry talked of everyday things I felt uneasy. The sun was shining, the familiar sounds of engines being tested could be heard, and yet when he had told me of the dream I had experienced that *frisson* at the nape of the neck which comes with reading ghost stories, or hearing the wind howl strangely at night.

Eventually the crews were summoned for a continuation of briefing. When everyone was sitting down the Vicar walked in. 'Well, chaps,' he began, 'there has been a change of target. Four crews will be disappointed because this is going to be a GH raid. The following crews will not fly today.' He read out four names and Dig's was first on the list.

And now Dig was looking at us, hoping that someone would explain convincingly why Harry had hunches.

It was Les who provided a solution. He suggested that the next time a battle-order was posted we should make sure that at all times until briefing someone was with Harry. In this way nobody would be able to approach Harry without our knowledge, and when the time for briefing arrived we would ask him to predict the target.

Nobody cared much for the test; it would prove nothing, and none of us thought that Harry was deliberately leaking information. On the other hand, his hunches were sometimes uncanny, and there comes a point when a series of predictions can no longer be dismissed as inspired guesses. We had reached that point. I disliked the idea of a test and said so, but Dig began to harden; he didn't think it would do any harm and if we could settle once and for all that Harry's hunches were harmless, he for one would feel a lot easier. There was some further inconclusive talk about the faculty of intuition, and everyone re-affirmed what a bloody good chap Harry was, and finally it was agreed to put Les's plan into operation when the next suitable opportunity occurred.

The crew was separated when the following battle-order was posted and the test was shelved for the time being. As briefing was not until the evening I rode into Bury St Edmunds to have a petrol leak on the bike repaired. After leaving the garage I wandered through the streets and finally went to the public library. It was a cold clear afternoon and the sun's rays shone through the windows on to the books I opened. I knew that at this moment each Lancaster was being fuelled with a maximum load of petrol and that this meant it would be a deep penetration raid, and I felt more restless and nervous than usual. Possibly my choice of books was an unconscious effort to establish a connection with an earlier, safer existence, because I found I was reading the poems I had enjoyed at school. But if it was some sort of security I sought the books failed to provide comfort, and I felt increasingly nervous.

The sun was low in the west on the ride back to camp and the eastern sky was darkening. In Germany it would already be night.

At the pre-flight meal everyone was trying to guess where the target would be. Harry said, 'Berlin maybe,' but he confessed he had no hunches about it.

79

Les and I walked up to the briefing room together.

On the wall map a long red ribbon began in Suffolk, dived down to Beachy Head, went south and east over France, south of Cologne, past Stuttgart, in between Frankfurt and Mannheim, north-east in the direction of Nuremberg, over unknown towns in the province of Saxony to a place called Döbeln from where there was a forty mile run-in to the target, Dresden.

Nobody had ever heard of Dresden being raided before and it was a safe bet that it would not be girdled by the black belt of defence worn by Ruhr cities or Berlin. I felt almost cheerful when the Bombing Leader walked round handing out flimsies which showed each Lancaster would be carrying one 4,000-pound Cookie and canisters of incendiaries.

Main briefing began and talk hushed into silence as crews sat squeezed on benches in front of tables covered with maps. Until recently, we were told, Dresden had been comparatively unimportant but since the recent advance of Russian troops the population of Dresden had been swollen by a million refugees. Conditions there were chaotic and ours was to be a panic raid adding confusion and disrupting communications. Up to eight hundred Lancasters would be operating and the attack was to be in two phases; our squadron was to reach the target towards the end of the second phase which was timed to start at 1.30 a.m. A Master Bomber would be present over the target to radio instructions to bomb-aimers. We were also told that although cloud lay over much of the Continent the sky should be clear above Dresden.

During the briefing I remembered newsreels taken early in the war and in my mind's eye saw a long stream of French refugees, their possessions piled on handcarts and prams, scattering in panic as bombs fell from Stuka dive-bombers. The memory was instant and vivid and left me feeling disturbed; and the recollection of that moment of memory is itself so vivid that it has never left me.

When briefing was finished we had time to waste before going by bus to A-Able's dispersal. I left the noise and smoke of the briefing room and went outside. The night was cool and tangled with stars. For a while I stood alone thinking of the journey ahead, of my home, and of Audrey.

On rejoining the others it seemed that they were all a trifle tense.

This would be by far the longest trip we had ever flown and would take us to within seventy miles of the advancing Russians, and it would mean that we should be in the air for nine hours.

Dig appeared with his hands full of chocolate, chewing gum and barley sugar.

'Here's your rations, mates,' he said.

'Milk chocolate for a change,' said Paul. This was a luxury; usually the chocolate was plain; but George looked apprehensive. Normally he exchanged his gum for Paul's chocolate and saved the chocolate for his younger brother. 'Don't you want to swap?' he asked.

One could see the conflict on Paul's face. He loved milk chocolate, but he had met George's brother. 'She's right, Kiddie,' he said. 'I'll swap.'

Dig handed out the escape kits and shortly after the bus was ready to take us to Able's dispersal.

I checked my guns and instruments while Dig and Ray warmed up the engines. It would be Able's first sortie since the landing at St Eval.

We took-off at 21.40 hours; the leaders of the first wave would by now be on the last lap of their flight to Dresden. I settled down in my compartment, not an easy task because the supply of 'window' occupied every spare inch, and adjusted to the boring flight over England. Suddenly I saw a Lancaster coming straight towards us on the starboard side. I shouted a warning and then the Lancaster vanished. It was a moment or two before I realized that my eyes had deceived me and I was thankful that my intercom had not been switched on and nobody had heard my panicky shout.

The night was dark but starlight was strong enough to throw the English coastline into relief. Able began to climb and by the time we had donned our oxygen masks, and Dig had changed into 'M' gear, we were over France. Cloud had formed and a vast whiteness lay below. I left my compartment, forced past Ray and sat beside Les. He was working the Gee and scribbling down figures; his shoulders seemed more hunched than usual. I flicked on the H2S switch. Pulses flickered and jumped on the screen. I tuned in and waited for earth returns.

Les said we were passing over the battle-lines and shortly afterwards the blips on his Gee became a writhing green band.

'Gerry's jammed Gee,' he reported to Dig, and, to me he said, 'Any luck, Mike?'

No luck, I told him.

A long silence followed as Able droned into the night.

Paul spoke suddenly. 'Flak to port.'

'Yeah, some to starboard too,' said Dig.

'Aye, that's right,' said Les. 'We'll be between Frankfurt and Mannheim.'

Ray began to grumble, or rather, he switched on his intercom to say two words. 'Bloody Mike,' he said.

'What now?' I asked.

'Only that while you're pretending to be useful I've got to push out "window". I'm expected to keep a log going, you know.'

'What is there to pushing a few bits of paper out?'

I made the question sound like a sneer and he jumped to the bait. 'Quite a bloody lot,' he retorted angrily, 'when you've got to keep on crawling into your compartment and crawling bloody out.'

'Help you to keep slim, old man.' This time I spoke in the laziest of Oxford accents which infuriated him. He told me to get knotted and chunnered about lazy bloody bomb-aimers who never did their work properly and were a dead bloody loss anyway.

When he had finished Les said, 'No joy, Mike?'

I shook my head. He reached out and dimmed the lights. 'Now turn up "Brilliance",' he said.

I turned up 'Brilliance.'

'Still no joy?'

I told him it was too mushy. Nuremberg should be within range but I couldn't identify it.

Dig who had been following the conversation said, 'There's flak way up front.'

Another long silence.

Les spoke, 'The Gee box is well and truly jammed. I haven't had a fix for more than an hour. Looks as though we'll be flying on dead reckoning tonight.'

'H2S and Gee both u/s?' It was Paul's voice.

'Still awake, Junior?' asked Dig.

'Not half. I'm bloody cold. This electric suit isn't working.'

Les sat back and looked at me. The oxygen mask covered his face to the bridge of his nose. Above it, his eyes gleamed. 'I'm going to have an easy time,' he said. 'Flying round on elementary navigation.'

Then we had a stroke of luck. The H2S cleared and I got a good fix on a town some ten miles ahead as a green blob floated down the line of flight marker. It could only be Döbeln, the town where we were to turn for the target run-in. Les checked his calculations against the fix and agreed.

I left the H2S set and wriggled past Ray into my compartment. Although we were forty miles from Dresden fires were reddening the sky ahead. The meteorological forecast had been correct. There was no cloud over the city.

Six miles from the target other Lancasters were clearly visible; their silhouettes black in the rosy glow. The streets of the city were a fantastic latticework of fire. It was as though one was looking down at the fiery outlines of a crossword puzzle; blazing streets stretched from east to west, from north to south, in a gigantic saturation of flame. I was completely awed by the spectacle. Then I heard Dig's voice. 'Where do you want me to go, Mike?'

There was no sound of the Master Bomber on the R/T.

I told Dig to turn to starboard, to the south of the city. He swung the aircraft away from the heart of the inferno and when we were just beyond the fringe of the fires I pressed the bomb release. I hoped the load would fall in open country; I couldn't forget what we had been told at briefing, or the old newsreels of German dive-bombing atrocities.

George's voice came through. 'Got a broadcast wind, Les.'

'Aye, Kiddie. Let's have it.'

'295 degrees, 65 m.p.h.'

'Thanks, Kiddie.'

'How does that compare with your winds, Les?' interjected Dig.

'Not so dusty, but I think I'll stick to mine.'

'Good on you. Keep it up.'

After a long spell of lying on my stomach 'windowing' I felt sleep enveloping me and told Les I would come back to try the H2S.

'Okay, I'll tune it up for you,' he said obligingly.

'So I've got to "window" again, have I?' Ray sensed that my only reason for going aft was to make life hard for him.

A thermos flask of coffee stood on Les's table and he poured out a cup for me. Our position on the chart seemed far too close to the target but he was reckoning on a stronger headwind than the broadcast wind.

'We're just passing over a big river,' said Dig.

The H2S screen gave blurred returns; it was impossible to identify any towns.

Harry chipped in. 'I can see that river Dig mentioned. There's a loop like a horseshoe on it' — a pause while he translated a glimmering loop of water into a navigational fix — 'at a bearing of 045 degrees and five miles.'

Les and I pored over the chart.

'It could be the Danube,' I said.

'That would make us twenty miles off track.'

I tried the H2S again and saw what could have been the serpentine line of a river. It seemed to confirm Harry's bearing. Les thought for a few moments and his eyes looked tired and worried. At last he said, 'I'll not use the fix. I don't think the wind has changed that much.'

Ray used the opportunity to score a point. 'You're no bloody use up there, Mike,' he said. 'Come and do a bit of work for a change. I'm fed up "windowing".'

I struggled back to my hole.

Able bored into the night. Time dragged by. Flak spurted up ahead and in the distance some searchlights coned a luckless Lancaster. The number of searchlights and the flak indicated a large town. I mentioned this to Les.

'Aye, that's Nuremberg,' he said with assurance.

'Nuremberg,' exclaimed the crew in unison.

'We must be past there, mate,' cajoled Dig.

'We're not, you know.'

'How many more miles to the Gerry border?' asked Paul.

'A couple of hundred,' replied Les in a sprightly voice.

A stream of red tracer curled ahead. Enemy fighters must be near by. I stood up and wormed myself into the cold front turret and checked my guns were on 'Fire'.

It seemed that eternities passed before Paul spoke again to ask if we were clear of the battle-lines yet.

'Not yet,' replied Les, 'just south of Stuttgart.' This was followed by a tuneless hum; no one told him to switch off his microphone. Our fate was in his hands to bring us home on dead reckoning.

Stuttgart. The town we had visited on the third operation months before, and that flight had seemed endless.

Fighter flares lobbed down in front like big slow-falling stars. There was a spate of talk; an enemy was prowling somewhere above.

The flares drifted behind and disappeared.

'We've passed the battle-lines,' said Les eventually.

The first weak light of day was wiping the slate of stars as we crossed the French coast. I emptied Dig's can for the third and last time.

'We're below ten thou,' said Dig, 'you can take off your oxygen masks.' He threw down a packet of menthol impregnated cigarettes at me. 'You have these. You like 'em, I don't.'

Gratefully I lighted a cigarette and inhaled. Usually we observed the no smoking rule but every so often it is pleasant to break rules made for one's own good by other people, and this was such an occasion.

We touched down at base nine hours and thirty-five minutes after taking off having covered approximately one thousand six hundred miles. It was a particular triumph for Les whose Gee set hadn't worked since shortly after passing the battle-lines on the way out. He had maintained a dogged faith in his own calculations in spite of different winds broadcast over the wireless, and a false fix from me.

All squadron aircraft returned safely and at interrogation crews spoke among themselves about the vast conflagration. Nobody had ever seen anything to compare with Dresden. There simply weren't the adjectives or comparisons available. It was like trying to describe a phenomenon never before witnessed by human eyes. Measurements and talk of 'a fantastic glow in the sky' didn't describe acre upon acre of streets and buildings ravaged by fire typhoons and the enormous bowl of rosy light which reached to altitudes unattainable by aircraft.[13]

We went to bed at nine in the morning immediately after breakfast. I slept for four hours and then washed, shaved and dressed, and started the motor-bike. Soon I should be meeting Audrey and I felt fine. On the way through camp I stopped at the Flight Office to make certain that the crew would not be required during the remainder of the day.

'Nothing on?' I said to an airman standing at the door.

'There is,' he said. 'A battle-order has gone up for tonight.'

A paper was pinned to the notice board; it contained a type-written list of names and our crew was named.

'It's a minimum bomb load again,' said someone. He spoke as though he found it hard to believe.

I went straight to the Mess and telephoned the Angel Hotel. I asked the receptionist to let Audrey know I might be late.

10. *The Test*

IN RETROSPECT I think it was at this point that I became something like a mercenary or professional soldier. The quiver of outrage at the briefing for Dresden and dropping the bombs clear of the periphery in the hope that they would fall harmlessly in fields was a last gesture to an ideal of common humanity. To be honest I am not sure which I found more distasteful − the idea of actually bombing refugees, or the idea that when the Allies were bombing refugees it was all right but when the Germans bombed refugees it was all wrong.

From the time a fresh battle-order was posted after the Dresden raid I realized I was paid to do a job, and I had to do that job. If I was damned, I was damned. I didn't care. Fear had nothing to do with professionalism. One was afraid when the job was dangerous but one didn't brood about fear when the danger was past. One had to expect private arrangements to be broken at a moment's notice and to forsake the prospect of sexual warmth for the chill of a cabin at twenty thousand feet, and to accept the change without rancour.

I had ceased counting the number of operations left in our extended tour. So far as I could see, we should go on flying until we were killed and there wasn't any point in teasing oneself with the prospect of ultimate safety. Having accepted the worst, it was easy to live for the best and for the moment. When one has reached this state, civilized ideals and cultural theories seem like so much hot air. It becomes crystal clear that man is basically a self-centred animal who has inherited an enormous legacy of aggressive impulses, and any idea that world peace can be permanently established by the civilized strivings of enlightened men and women seems as likely to succeed as a movement seeking to ban orgasm from all sexual encounters.

War itself does not brutalize men; war is simply a state of

existence. Men are 'brutalized' by the defence mechanisms of their own minds when the dreadful results of war (sudden death of comrades, maimed bodies) can no longer be coped with on a civilized level of natural empathy. Men and women cannot sustain indefinitely a high intensity of shocked horror while continuing to participate in the action causing the horror. It is here that the mind comes to the rescue, and it may be a part of the instinct of survival that 'brutalizes' men and makes them indifferent to the suffering of others.

These few thoughts were not in my mind as I rode from the Mess to the hut to bring the crew news of another operation (few men have a revelation on the road to Damascus) but I think that the condition which I have attempted to describe was rapidly evolving in my subconscious mind whilst on the surface of my mind I was able to shrug off the disappointment of not meeting Audrey.

Within the hut there was a scene of unfamiliar orderliness. The crew were resplendent in best blue, and brass buttons shone with intentions for a bright night out in town. George, Les and Paul were already groomed and were waiting for Ray who was polishing shoes that already twinkled. Only Harry, sitting on his bed, was wearing battle-dress. Had he guessed that there was no purpose in getting dressed for town?

'Why are you back, Mike?' asked Les.

'What's the matter?' asked George.

Paul guessed the answer. 'We're on,' he said.

Ray looked up from his shoes. 'Oh, boy,' he said wearily.

I told them it was another minimum bomb load and that we were down to fly in A-Able. While I was speaking Les caught my eye and tipped his head slightly in Harry's direction.

'Harry,' I said, 'the boys don't understand your hunches. You get the gen from inside your head, nowhere else, don't you?'

'You know I do,' he said. He looked at the others. 'Everything must be explained, eh? I'd be angry if I wasn't amused.' He laughed to show amusement, but we all looked uncomfortable.

'No offence, lad,' said Les.

Paul went across the hut and sat down beside Harry. 'You must admit it's hard for ignorant bastards like me to understand these things. Blokes like me, Kiddie and Les aren't trying to be clever. We're just curious.'

For Paul this was something of a speech. Harry gave him a long, amused look and said, 'You're all right, Junior.'

There was some general talk about the complexity of the human brain and how little anyone understood of its processes; then Paul asked, 'Where do you reckon we're going tonight, Harry?'

'Berlin, I hope.'

(For some extraordinary reason Harry had always wanted to pay one visit to Berlin.)

George went to look for Dig to make sure he knew about tonight's flight, and Les suggested we had a few games of bridge.

Right until time for briefing Harry was with two or three members of the crew. Take-off was scheduled for 20.00 hours and I went to the briefing room as soon as it was open. On the wall the red ribbon led to a town about forty miles to the west of Dresden. I had never heard of the place as a target and I doubted whether Harry had either.

Having noted the objective I went to the adjoining room where Dig and the others were waiting. I think that by this time Harry knew that he was at the centre of a plot, but he didn't know its nature. I had mixed feelings; I wanted him to prove that he did possess some sort of precognitive power because this would show that any leakage of target information was not being fed through him. On the other hand, I felt that by becoming involved in the plot I was betraying our friendship.

The crew looked at me. I decided I couldn't pose the fateful question and simply said, 'Not much sleep for us tonight.'

It was Dig who turned to Harry and said, 'Have a shot at guessing the target, mate.'

At this point I think Harry realized it was more than a plot; it was a trial. He moved across to where a map of Europe was pinned to the wall. It was a smaller edition of the briefing room map and was unmarked by any ribbon.

He put out his hand and let it stray across the map until his forefinger reached Leipzig; then he moved it across the province of

Brandenberg. He paused and his finger began to move towards Chemnitz where it stopped. Had he been giving a stage performance it could not have been more theatrically effective.

'It might be Leipzig, or perhaps Brandenberg, or even Chemnitz...I think it'll be Chemnitz,' he said.

The crew looked at me. I alone knew what the target was. 'He's right,' I said.

For a moment Dig looked stunned, then he said 'Christ!' turned and walked out of the room and into the briefing room as though he must check for himself that I was telling the truth.

Harry was upset. 'What is all this?' he asked.

Nobody could give an adequate reply.

It was an uneasy crew that assembled to hear main briefing. Chemnitz, we were told, was crammed with refugees who had managed to escape from the previous night's holocaust and again we were to spread chaos by bombing this place already made chaotic by the huge influx of refugees. If the attack was as successful as the attack on Dresden, it was unlikely that we should be paying any more visits to the Russian front. I listened without any qualms. I was far more concerned that Harry was sitting as far from the rest of us as he could manage without appearing to belong to a different crew. And yet, from the abstract application of ethics and morality, as distinct from the practical consideration of helping the Russian advance, the raid on Chemnitz was probably less justifiable, and more inhuman than the Dresden raid.

We were told that diversions would be staged by Mosquito squadrons to draw off enemy fighters. There would be two separate phases of attack; our squadron would reach the target at the end of the second phase. A Master Bomber would be present to give directions. More than three hundred bomber aircraft would take part in each phase.

Briefing finished with the Vicar's customary 'Good luck, chaps, and when you come back don't let there be a Chemnitz.'

Dig went to collect flying rations. On his return, and while I was helping him to count them into seven equal piles, Harry came up and tugged at my shoulder to attract attention. I didn't turn at once.

'Look,' he said, suddenly before me, 'If you weren't going on ops tonight, I'd knock you down!'

He strode away with such a swagger of aggression that the loose straps of his parachute harness slapped against his thighs.

'What was that for?' asked Dig.

I didn't know, but guessed that Harry was furious with me for having taken part in the test.

The route to Chemnitz was similar to the Dresden route. Mechanics had repaired the defect in Les's Gee but had marked the H_2S as temporarily unserviceable.

Over the Continent, layers of cloud stretched from the French coast to East Germany and over Chemnitz Pathfinder flares disappeared almost as soon as they were dropped. The voice of the Master Bomber, a Canadian, came clearly over the R/T. He kept calling for more flares, but few were forthcoming. He seemed to have little idea of where to direct the bomber stream. Eventually he gave up his appeals for flares in disgust. 'Oh, hell,' he said. 'I'm going home. See you at breakfast.'

In front, a Lancaster dropped some parachute flares and I decided I might as well bomb on these. I began calling corrections to Dig. As though unaware of the proximity of the target Harry began to chatter.

'Shut up,' said Dig.

'Who the hell are you talking to?' Harry was indignant.

'Shut up,' shouted Dig.

'No man tells me to shut up.'

'Bombs gone,' I said.

'Were you on the run-up, Mike?' There was surprise and uncertainty in Harry's voice.

'I was.'

'Sorry — Mike.' The emphasis on my name implied that he was not apologizing to Dig.

Dig spoke slowly like a man who finds it an effort to retain his self-control. 'A — bloody — poor — show,' he said. 'Well...'

'Forget it,' said Dig abruptly.

Les provided a new course and this averted more argument.

Once again we struggled home against strong headwinds. Everyone was tired; there were long silences.

Then without any warning Harry began to blaze away with his machine-guns. A JU88 had appeared about two hundred yards from our tail. His burst frightened it off. There was a brief splatter of excitement which ended as suddenly as it had begun. The stale smell of cordite drifted into the front compartments.

We landed at 4.45 a.m., having been airborne eight hours and twenty minutes.

I was with Audrey before daylight and had taken the precaution of bringing some 'wakey-wakey pills' (benzedrine tablets officially issued to aircrew) with me. It seemed wasteful to go to bed with an attractive woman and then promptly fall asleep; but I was so tired I didn't trust myself to stay awake without stimulants. The benzedrine worked well, but by the time I returned to camp in the evening I felt I could sleep enough for two lifetimes.

On the following day I went to the officers' quarters and Dig and I sat in his small bedroom which was only slightly better furnished than our hut. I told him that Harry was still unhappy about the 'test' and the incident over the target at Chemnitz. After some discussion Dig agreed to call the crew together to thrash things out. There followed a meeting in the hut at the end of which he and Harry shook hands. Nobody referred to hunches, or intuition, again, and Harry never attempted another prophecy.

11. *What the Hell are We Fighting For?*

HALF A DOZEN West Indian Aircraftsmen (Second Class) worked on the squadron. There was no third class of aircraftsman; the second class aircraftsman was, in the words beloved by generations of warrant officers, the lowest form of Air Force life. One day, a West Indian detailed to empty a dustbin, tipped its contents on the middle of a plot of grass by the Orderly Room. No one had told him where dustbins should be emptied and he had thought this looked a suitable place. He was told he was a horrible airman and that he should never tip dustbins by the Orderly Room. Having no wish other than to please he carefully placed the contents of his next dustbin in the centre of the lawn by the adjutant's office. He was charged with disobeying orders.

He came to Harry and begged Harry to speak in his defence. It was a brief Harry accepted with pleasure, and he was furious to learn, after returning from Chemnitz, that the West Indian had been sentenced to seven days' jankers while he, Harry, was sleeping off the effects of a long night flight. Not only was his sense of justice outraged but he held a special position in the eyes of his compatriots (somewhere between King George VI and God) and he felt he owed it to himself and to them to protest about the sentence.

His form of protest was novel. He spoke bitterly and at length about the injustice of the case in the presence of the Station Warrant Officer, and poured scorn on all forms of authority until the Station Warrant Officer was left with no alternative but to charge Harry with conduct prejudicial to good order and discipline.

He was duly marched, under escort, to the Vicar who, as was customary, gave him the choice of accepting a sentence there and then or going before a higher authority with greater punitive powers. Harry elected to appear before the higher authority. His stand caused a small sensation in the Mess and a number of brave spirits informed him that, were they in his shoes, they would take on the Group, the Command, and the whole of Air Ministry itself in defence of their principles.

Harry returned to the hut and composed a six-page defence of the man who had been sentenced to jankers. It was a rhetorical document which owed something to Abraham Lincoln and something to the causes of the French Revolution, but just as he was about to be taken before the Group Captain a rush battle-order was posted. Harry's declaration on the rights of man would have to wait.

It was a spring morning with clear blue skies when the crew took-off in A-Able to bomb a small town on the Rhine. Hitler's fanatical bid for Antwerp and Brussels in the battle of the Ardennes had failed. For a few weeks the Allied troops had been satisfied to rest along the lines of the river Meuse; then on the eighth of February an assault on the Rhineland began. British troops managed to gain a front lying approximately between Nijmegen-Cleve-Goch. Farther north, the Canadians had fought to the west bank of the Rhine opposite Emmerich, and in the south the United States First Army were lining the river Roer. It was now essential to bring Allied armies up to a focal bridging point on the Rhine. The inhabitants of Wesel were to discover that by a wretched historical chance they occupied a kernel which lay firmly between nutcrackers.

For the greater part of the war Wesel's military importance was negligible; the only possible strategic objective it contained was a railway siding. But now it was filled with German troops travelling to and from the western front and consequently Bomber Command had been ordered to reduce it to rubble. Such a small town presented a limited target area and, since Allied soldiers were closing in, it was decreed that the bombing should be undertaken by GH crew to ensure the highest degree of accuracy.

As we approached the battle-lines the thin white vapour trails of V2s being launched far to the north could be seen. The sky above Wesel was of purest blue marred only by sparse black blobs. Obviously the anti-aircraft defences were not very strong but they claimed one victim when a Lancaster flying ahead of us exploded into a vast balloon of oil and flame. But apart from this casualty all aircraft returned safely and we all agreed when George wistfully remarked, 'We could do with some more like that.'[14]

George's wish was granted. We were briefed to bomb Wesel again on the following day and Harry's trial was postponed once more. On this trip a Flight Sergeant pilot came as second dickie and his enthusiasm to start on ops was almost touching; as was the dedication of his crew of sergeants all of whom turned out to shiver at the end of the runway to see him off. As Dig opened up Able's throttles for take-off the little group of sergeants waved furiously and their mouths were opened wide in shouts and cheers which were lost in the roar of Able's engines.

It was another easy sortie and, as was his habit recently, Dig flew back low over the sea, soared to a thousand feet over the English coast and then swooped to brush East Anglia just above the treetops. On the previous day he had dived at a bridge and two elderly ladies had ducked behind the parapet; today he flew Able along a straight road and a man riding a push bike turned his head to look round and then fell off his bike in fright. Dig said later that it was the funniest thing he had ever seen.

That evening Les heard the second dickie boasting to his men. 'Pukka operational crew' he had said, 'the bomb-aimer was asleep till we reached the target, and the skipper did some nifty low flying on the way back.' It was nice to think that he attributed my drowsiness to sang-froid.

Harry, who had fretted to speak his piece for two days and during two raids, was on the third day taken before the Group Captain. He emerged bewildered from the Group Captain's office. He had not been allowed to read his plea; instead, he had been hustled in, formally charged, sentenced to have a severe reprimand entered on his records, and hustled out. He was almost speechless with the indignity of the procedure but wisely ignored advice lavished on him by the brave spirits in the Mess.

When the crew heard of Harry's sentence and saw him sitting forlornly holding six pages he had never read, the question was raised, 'What the hell are we fighting for?'

A West Indian had unintentionally disobeyed orders and had not been allowed to have a second West Indian speak on his behalf. The second West Indian had protested and not been allowed to explain the reasons for his protest. And yet both men were fighting for Britain and to preserve liberty, including the right of free speech.

It was the second half of February and the ground was no longer iron hard underfoot. The hours of daylight were stretching like limbs, throwing off the shackles of winter. Birds were singing and, on the squadron, like the first buds of spring, the faces of new flyers appeared. The training bottleneck had eased and fresh crews were being pumped into squadrons all over England.

The Wesel raids had been on a Sunday and Monday. On Tuesday, with another second dickie, a dark-complexioned Flying Officer with a scar on his face, we were briefed for a daylight raid on a benzol plant at Gelsenkirchen. It was to be a dash in from the north-west and a dash out in the same direction, but after briefing the operation was cancelled.

On Wednesday we were again briefed for the same target by the same route and again the raid was cancelled. The crew of young sergeants, anxious to begin their tour, left the briefing room feeling very frustrated, as did another new crew led by an officer who looked too young to drive a car, let alone fly an aeroplane.

On Thursday we were briefed for the same target, the Alma Pluto Benzol plant at Gelsenkirchen, but this time, after bombing, we were to turn south-west and fly over Essen and Krefeld. It seemed a crazy flight plan for a daylight operation, even if the route was covered by cloud. And why, if it was suspected that the enemy were being informed in advance of targets, had we been briefed to fly to the same place on three consecutive mornings?

Our new second dickie was nervous. He smoked incessantly and for no apparent reason singled me out for company and conversation. I learned that his face had been scarred in a car crash and that his wife was expecting their first child. He questioned me about raids, asking what it was like to be under fire, what targets were good and what bad, and then he would talk about his wife. He sat next to me during briefing and listened intently, as did everyone; crews wanted to know

96

A-Able returning after first night raid on Neuss

Klenner's crew on 21st June 1944 before starting ops and before being joined by Flight Engineer (*standing l to r*) 'Mike', Paul, George (*seated l to r*) 'Dig', Harry, Les

Klenner's crew on 11th March 1945 after completing ops. (*News Chronicle*) (*l to r*) 'Mike', Ray, George, 'Dig', Paul, Les, Harry

The squadron airfield at Chedburgh, Suffolk. To the untrained eye
it was exactly like hundreds of other airfields, but to squadron crews,
returning from a raid, it was uniquely appealing.

why this extraordinary route had been chosen. The Meteorological Officer tried to allay doubts by stating that the Ruhr was entirely covered by thick cumulus cloud. His information was greeted with muttered scepticism. But when the Intelligence Officer said that the opposition would be so astounded by the unorthodox route that by the time they recovered from the shock we should be out of range, he was met with hoots of disbelief and derision. He grinned back at the crews and sat down.

We boarded the bus and during the wait at dispersal the second dickie continued to talk about his pregnant wife and the trip ahead. When we climbed aboard he stood behind Ray and I went into the nose for take-off. From time to time during the flight I turned and gave him a thumbs-up and he nodded back. Then Dig asked for his can and during the next few seconds A-Able began to dive gently towards the tail turret of a Lancaster in front. I turned as the second dickie was reaching anxiously for the control column. Dig came through on the intercom with the words, 'She's right, mate,' as he passed the can with one hand and pulled up Able's nose with the other.

The meteorological forecast was wrong. It was a cloudless sky over the Ruhr. We approached Gelsenkirchen in a hailstorm of flak and from the patter of fragments I knew we had been hit. The bomb doors were open and our cargo was exposed; it needed only a fragment of flak to detonate a bomb and the second dickie's worries, and all our worries, would be over. I wondered how the two new crews were faring. The Flight Sergeant whom we had taken to Wesel was flying with his crew of sergeants in a new C-Charlie, but I couldn't see them anywhere. Over to port a Lancaster fell in a sheet of flame.

Dig was weaving the aircraft slightly as Les gave the count-down. When the bombs wobbled dizzily away he swerved violently on to a new course. The enormous conurbation of the Ruhr below and ahead was spread out like a large-scale topographical map. I picked out the industrial complex of Essen and as we flew towards it the Essen defences opened fire. One of the leading Lancasters went down like a shot bird and then Able was hit again, close to the wing roots on the starboard side. The engineer's panel was ripped open and the petrol gauges for the port side engines fell to zero. The second dickie was crouching on all fours on the floor.

Leaving Essen the silver Rhine lay ahead like a snake on a quilt. We flew between Duisburg and Düsseldorf and into the black-smudged sky above Krefeld. Dig said, 'To hell with briefed airspeeds,' and opened the throttles wide. We began to overtake other bombers but it was some time before we were clear of flak; the stream was harried for some miles by guns mounted on rolling stock.

When we were clear Dig asked whether anyone had seen C-Charlie over the target area. No one had. It sounds ridiculous to say that one has a protective instinct towards a crew flying on their maiden operation simply because their skipper gained his first operational experience flying as Dig's co-pilot, but it was something akin to this, and we were concerned about the fate of C-Charlie. We didn't think once about the other new crew led by the officer who looked like a fifth-form schoolboy.

On leaving France Dig skimmed the North Sea. It was a brilliant piece of low flying. In the bomb-aimer's compartment the water's surface seemed close enough to touch; but I wished he wasn't performing with a damaged aircraft. Glancing back I saw that the second dickie had gone aft so I decided to clamber up and stand behind Ray and Dig. Racing water under one's eyes can induce a sort of visual nausea.

When we reached the coast Dig put Able into a climb. I looked back and saw the second dickie's head in the astrodome; his oxygen mask dangled by his scar and his face was pallid. Then Dig dived the aircraft again and we were skimming flat green countryside. Suddenly he noticed a bus trundling along a country road; forward went the stick, the bus raced towards us, and at the last moment we zoomed up again.

The second dickie's face was now white and his lips were repeating the words, 'You bastard...You bastard....' I didn't blame him for being frightened; I had been frightened too. I said to Dig, 'You've got a bloody nerve to treat a damaged kite like that.'

He looked up at me, and grinned. 'This is Able, my friend,' he said.

Over base we noticed that Charlie's dispersal was empty and there was no sound of the pilot among the clamour of returning pilots on the R/T.

98

Dig landed, and at the intersection of runways turned right to taxi to Able's dispersal. An airman guided him on to the concrete apron and when he signalled a criss-cross with his arms Dig cut the engines.

An absolute silence followed and perhaps for five seconds no one moved or spoke. This was the moment of adjustment at the end of a trip when muscles relaxed and one's eyes recognized airfield landmarks. It was the time of stability after instability, and the time of reconnection with normal life. It was a brief pause but, in its way, as necessary as food or sleep. Then we began gathering parachute packs, flimsies and maps, and rather stiffly clambered towards the exit by the tail. We were waiting for the bus when a Lancaster, three airscrews whirling and one rigid, came in to land directly above us. 'It's Charlie!' shouted Paul, and began to wave.

But the other new crew failed to return and on the following day a little tragedy was posted on the squadron notice boards. Under the heading 'New Arrivals' seven names were listed, and directly below, under the heading 'Missing in Action' were the same seven names.[15]

In the Mess that evening Jock Henderson told us that if one of the flak fragments had hit the aircraft an inch higher or lower its undercarriage would have collapsed on landing.

'What about Able herself?' asked Les. 'When will she be fit to fly again?'

'She could be ready within the week,' replied Jock, 'but she's in bloody poor state. It's time for a major overhaul anyway. I'm damned if I know how she flies now. Yesterday I changed the flame traps on the port inner; they were solid with muck. The other traps aren't any better. That alone makes her technically unserviceable.'

'Do your best, Jock,' said Les. 'We want to finish the tour on her. We don't fancy another aircraft now.'

'Aye, I know how it is. But I can't see her standing many more trips as she is. How many are there left?'

Les thought for a moment. 'Nine,' he said.

Jock shook his head. 'She canna make it.'

Someone else was not going to make it either. Audrey was to be discharged from the W.A.A.F. on medical grounds. She had joined in 1940 when she was eighteen and for the past five years the Air Force had been her life, and it was a life she loved. She intended to go home to her widowed mother in Liverpool, but after that her future was uncertain. Her discharge was to take effect almost immediately.

After a day's inactivity we flew in P-Peter to bomb a synthetic oil plant at Kamen near Dortmund. Dig pronounced that Peter was a beaut to fly and took us four thousand feet above the other Lancasters after leaving the target. We had the mixed pleasure of watching predicted flak worrying the other bombers flying at the briefed height of eighteen thousand feet.

Once again Dig flew low over the North Sea, reared up over the English coast and, once inland, dived steeply again. He had seen a football match and as he dived the players stopped playing and we saw their faces, and the spectators' faces, looking up at us. I glanced ahead. We were heading straight for a tree-lined escarpment which rose steeply behind the football-ground. Dig saw it too, but a second too late. He wrenched the stick back, and the Lancaster bucked, but not high enough to clear the treetops. Of all our collectively lucky escapes, this was the luckiest. The Lancaster flew between two trees. Had its nose been pointing a few yards on either side we should have flown no more.

I was too shaken to speak, but Paul came through with, 'Christ, that was close, Dig!'

Ray said, 'Blimey, what's happening?' and the incident took a slightly comic turn because it appeared that during the shoot-up he had been crouching down reading the instruments on his panel and had glanced up to see tree branches flashing by. 'It's a bloody funny sensation,' he said, 'when all you expect to see is clouds.'

Later, when Dig and I were alone, I asked him to stop low flying. My nerves wouldn't stand any more. 'Don't worry, mate,' he replied. 'There won't be any more. I shit blue lights today.'

That evening I went to the Angel Hotel. Audrey arrived with two aircrew sergeants from the squadron where she had been stationed. The four of us had drinks in the bar and I heard that they had been among the Lancasters which had been chivvied by flak after leaving Kamen earlier in the day. Audrey listened quite happily to this 'shop' and insisted on buying a round of drinks. At the time I didn't realize how much this little session in a hotel bar, with three men comparing notes about flying, meant to her. But it was her farewell party. Eventually the sergeants left to return to their squadron. They shook hands with Audrey and me, and that was the end of the party.

I took Audrey to the station the next day and she boarded a train for Liverpool. She planned to spend a week with her mother before returning to Bury St Edmunds where she would remain until my tour was completed. In the meanwhile, I would try to get a room in a boarding-house. On my pay it was too expensive to stay every night at the Angel Hotel, although we had become fond of the place and were treated by the staff with a kindness which went far beyond the requirements of good hotel hospitality.

12. 'This is Good-bye to Able'

ON THE 27th February we flew in A-Able to bomb a benzol plant near Gelsenkirchen and on the following day, again in Able, we bombed the Nordstern benzol plant at Gelsenkirchen. On both trips there was some troublesome flak on the run-in.

On the 1st March we had a day's stand-down. The war was drawing to a close but I wasn't aware of this. Having learned to live in the present, the future was as opaque as a drift of cirrostratus and the past was a vanished city covered with cumulus. I flew on in the limited space between cloud layers and life was lived through the senses, sharpened by a desire for survival and wonderfully uncluttered by the dragging friction of the intellect.

Taste was the taste of a cigarette after hours of chewing gum, the taste of bacon and egg before an operation and baked beans after — you were never given beans before an operation in case you developed wind pains. Taste was also petrol sucked through a rubber tube from R.A.F. vehicles and rum at interrogation. Smell was coke fumes from the hut stove, aircraft dope, glycol, overheated flying-suits, the Suffolk air with its hints of salt sea breeze and pine, toasted bread and the peculiar interior odour of Lancasters. Touch was the feel of toes spreading in the warmth of fur-lined flying-boots, handlebars vibrating from a motor-bike at speed, the three gloves (silk, wool and leather) on each hand, the keys of a piano, the texture of long hair, the feel of all sorts of paper. Hearing was the sonorous roar of aero-engines, the Scots of Jock Henderson, Audrey's chuckle, Dig's digger talk, the Yorkshire of George and Les, the modified scouse of Paul, the Norfolk of Ray and the accent of a man who came from the Half Way Tree district of Kingston, Jamaica. Sight was the sky in every colour of the spectrum, the airfield environs, the façade of the

Angel Hotel, and every glittering oil-iridescent puddle in the gutter.

Flying an extra ten operations didn't change anyone's character but it accentuated characteristics. Paul had become more restless and erratic, George more elated and melancholic by turns, Ray more aggressive, Dig more of a leader than an equal, and Harry more amusingly cynical and touchy. Only Les remained much the same, reliable and reasonable, and I envied his unruffled demeanour and quiet efficiency. An indifference to the virtues of compassion, tolerance and charity had hardened within me, and these qualities in others were almost intolerable.

I didn't realize that the life we lived was limited in time, and that the time was running out. I continued to live in an eternal-seeming Now of the senses, a sort of primeval joy of wonder.

On the second day of March we were briefed to bomb Cologne. After each raid on this city newspapers proclaimed that it was dead but when we were briefed for our fourth raid it seemed that Cologne was a phoenix symbol of eternal resurrection. The defences, we were told, consisted of four hundred and fifty guns; it didn't require much imagination to think what this number could do to a square mile of sky. We were instructed to bomb on GH but, if GH was unserviceable, we must on no account bomb visually. Throughout briefing it was stressed that there must be no visual bombing.

When we were airborne, again in Able although she was flying very sluggishly, I remarked that bomb-aimers were just about obsolete.

'They never have been a deal of use, have they, mate?' asked Dig.

'All washed-out pilots,' added Paul.

'No bloody use at all,' said Ray.

As we neared Germany I felt increasingly nervous. It was a clear afternoon and, from below, the stream of about one hundred and fifty Lancasters must have looked like a horde of minnows swimming through pure blue water. Then, when we were in sight of Cologne, Les called, 'GH is u/s. We can't bomb.'

The city lay like exposed ganglia and nerve-ends on a plate. It was a perfect target, but not a single bomb fell from the bombers and, incredibly, not a single anti-aircraft gun opened fire. It was as though we were taking part in some peace-time air pageant as the Lancasters flew unharmed and unharming over Cologne and wheeled in a smooth curve on to the course for home.

'Give me five more like that,' said Paul.

Two days later we visited Wanne-Eickel in daylight to destroy a coking plant. Able's engines were running roughly and, although flak jumped like fleas leaping up from a sheep's pelt of cloud, Dig and Ray were more worried about maintaining height than being hit.

Jock Henderson and his mechanics were as usual awaiting Able's return but after he had spoken with Dig he said that another four trips without a major overhaul for Able were out of the question. He wanted to mark Able as unserviceable but Dig reminded him that there were no spare aircraft available on the squadron, and that we didn't want to stand down or fly in a different aircraft. At last, with his face like the Lowlands on a rainy afternoon, Jock agreed to pass Able as serviceable, but it was a decision which obviously went against both his conscience and his pride as an engineer.

As we flew to Gelsenkirchen on the following morning to bomb a benzol plant it became clear that Jock was right, and Able should have been condemned as unserviceable. Another second dickie – a taciturn Australian who would have made a good rugby lock forward – sat beside Dig and watched other Lancasters pulling away until Able was last in the stream and finally, as the battle-lines drew near, the only bomber in sight. I don't know what he was thinking as he heard Les giving revised estimates of the time of arrival at Gelsenkirchen when each estimate was later than the previous one, or how he felt when Dig said sadly, 'This kite is really crook,' but in the silences made fraught by the grumble of labouring pistons I wondered anxiously when Dig was going to decide to turn back.

A-Able tracked over the dark bruise of Wesel and into Germany. Visibility ahead was perfect; we should be giving the ground gunners some excellent target practice.

Dig spoke. He had made his decision. 'Well, mates,' he said, 'if we press on there'll only be three left to do...So...We press on.'

Paul said, 'That's the stuff, Dig. Fuck 'em all!'

No one else spoke. I thought of home, of God, of Audrey, of my parents, and I touched each of my lucky charms in turn.

The silence became so oppressive that I switched on the microphone and said that when we got back I was going to Bury for a haircut.

Immediately the aircraft was alive with good-natured ridicule; even

Ray's eyes creased above the rim of his oxygen mask. 'Mind you don't catch cold,' he said.

As we neared Gelsenkirchen we could see a thin, but widely spread, layer of cloud ahead. As the first tendrils curled round Able's wings the whipcrack of flak could be heard above the engines. The bursts continued during the run-in and just after the last bomb fell clear a tremendous explosion on the starboard side rocked Able from stem to stern. Dig slammed the controls forward and dived a few hundred feet into open sky before bringing up the aircraft's nose in a tight 180-degree climbing turn. He called up each of the crew in turn to make sure no one had been hurt.

Ray said, 'We've got to feather the starboard outer,' as Able regained the sanctuary of cloud.

When the blades had become a crucifix hanging on the damaged wing Dig said, 'Give me a course straight back to base, Les. To hell with the flight plan.'

Loss of the starboard outer meant loss of power for Paul's turret and, since single bombers are vulnerable to roving enemy fighters, I manned the front turret as Able flew in a direct line from Gelsenkirchen to a point in Suffolk.

Hardly anyone spoke on the return journey but as we passed over Holland Dig said, 'This is good-bye to Able,' and he sounded as though he was speaking of his dearest friend.

At base there was no palaver over the R/T, no tossing up and down of landing patter, no routine circuit, Dig simply said, 'Beany Able to Roughedge, I'm on three engines and must land,' and Control answered immediately, 'Pancake Able.'

Dig let Able sink lower and lower until the wheels touched the runway so lightly that the aircraft might have been a giant feather borne to earth on a breeze. All the crew agreed that his last landing in Able was the best he had ever made.

After interrogation the Vicar congratulated him. 'A magnificent press-on effort, old chap,' he said.

The pressure increased. We had flown five operations within a week and had been on almost continuous daily stand-bys or briefings for nearly a month. It was no surprise to find another battle-order posted on the following day. Lancaster D-Dog had been allocated to the crew and the target was a pre-dawn attack on what was left of Wesel. It was to be an Army support operation by a small force of Lancasters. The ruined town was filled with German troops.[16]

As Dig stepped off the bus at D-Dog's dispersal he gave a delighted shout. We saw Jock Henderson standing in the shadows.

'Thought you were on pass, Jock,' said Les as we crowded round him.

The Scotsman looked embarrassed. 'Aye, but I was spending it in camp and I no liked the thought of Dig warming up without me. Anyway, I couldn't sleep if I tried.'

We bombed Wesel through cloud and landed five and a half hours later.

At interrogation the Vicar informed us that there was to be another operation that night but since it was to be a long-distance raid he would omit us from the battle-order so that our tour could be concluded with a couple of easy flights. It was a nice gesture but we couldn't help remembering Evers's last easy operation.[17]

Nicky was back from Sheffield and in an unrepentant mood. Men on the discipline course were allowed out of camp each evening between 6 p.m. and 9 p.m. and would be met at the gates by women who wheeled prams full of bottled beer. Nicky had received letters and parcels from the widow who ran a tobacconist's shop and with these, and the pram-pushing women, he said he was aching to be disciplined again.

Crews were briefed to bomb a benzol plant at Datteln in the Ruhr and we were given K-King, an aircraft which had just received a major overhaul, not been air-tested, and had been bombed-up in the hangar while mechanics were still working on it.

The sun was shining and Paul suggested we should have a photograph taken. He chalked in huge letters '2 TO GO' on K-King's fuselage and we stood in a line while someone clicked a camera shutter. The superstitious side of my nature felt it was foolish to fly in an aircraft with such a message blazoned on its side; it was cocking a snook at Fate, luck, Providence and all the other notions to which the most rational of men will sometimes attribute their misfortunes. But I said nothing; I didn't want to be laughed at or for anyone to think I had 'the twitch' or was becoming 'flak happy'.

We had a second dickie passenger, a brisk and bustling Flight Lieutenant. He was stout and uncommendably keen. In turn he questioned each crew member about his particular pre-flight check. I was in no mood for his officious questions – he knew all the answers and was simply checking our efficiency – and when he said, 'Now then, bomb-aimer, tell me what you do,' I asked him to accompany me.

We stood together under K-King's belly. The bomb doors were open and above our heads were rows of neatly stacked bombs. I placed my arms round the nose of a 500-pound bomb and pulled up until my feet were off the ground and my whole weight supported by the bomb. 'If one bomb is secure, I reckon the rest are,' I said.

He gave me a peculiar look, said 'Really?' and walked swiftly away. Harry, who had been watching the performance and laughing quietly in the background, came across. 'You bloody line-shooter,' he said. He was right. I had been showing off. But I was also proving to myself that although the words chalked up by Paul had made me uneasy I wasn't afraid to take a risk. And, of course, it is always pleasurable to deflate men who insist on thrusting their egos at everyone.

But the second dickie got his revenge. He asked Dig if he could stand where I usually stood on take-off, just behind Ray. This request placed Dig in a difficult position. He was expected to give second dickies every possible assistance, but on the other hand he didn't want to upset me. He said, 'Do you mind, Mike?'

I was in the mood to say, 'I don't give a shit,' and so I said it.

Dig was obviously relieved. 'Good on you,' he said.

I went into the nose but any sense of throwaway recklessness vanished the moment Dig began the take-off. K-King slewed violently to the left. Dig braked, and while still moving forward at a fair speed, slowly straightened the aircraft. Lying on my stomach in the nose I could see that we had already used up too much runway for safety and I expected Dig to start slowing down so that he could taxi round the perimeter and make a second attempt. But instead, he advanced the throttles. A quick glance to the right showed we were half-way down a short runway and not moving at more than about forty miles an hour. As the aircraft began tardily to gain speed I could see the point where the runway ended and grass field began. A hedge lay about fifty yards beyond.

'Tittie for Christ's sake,' Dig called.

Ray pulled the automatic boost cut-out lever and a surge of power ran through K-King, but we were at the runway's end and only Harry in the tail was airborne. The hedge was racing towards us. This was to be the Stirling crash all over again except that this time we were increasing speed and we had a 13,000-pound bomb load.

King's wheels were kissing the grass as Dig said 'Undercart up.'

We were over the hedge and a tree raced by beneath.

'2850,' said Dig.

'2850,' Ray repeated.

I realized suddenly that instead of lying on my stomach I was bracing my body against the back of the compartment, my knees drawn up and my elbows tucked in tight in a huddle of fright. I couldn't remember how I had got into this position.

I said, 'If anyone wants a thrill they can change places with me on the next take-off.'

Dig ducked his head to look down. He was laughing. 'Sorry, Mike,' he said. 'It won't happen again.'

Dig's latest girl-friend was a WAAF working in the Control Tower, and Paul came through to say, 'Blow a skipper who has to frighten his poor bloody crew just because his girl is watching.'

'Apologies everyone,' laughed Dig.

The second dickie looked pale and he didn't ask a single question, or speak, throughout the entire trip. After the take-off, the operation was something of an anti-climax; my quota of fear for the day seemed to have been exhausted and I felt no qualms as we flew into a flak barrage. We landed five hours and twenty minutes after take-off.

That evening and the whole of the following day I spent with Audrey, but during the afternoon I met Les, George and Ray in Bury and learned that we were on a battle-order for the following day. I decided to be with Audrey for as much of the night as was possible and said, 'This time tomorrow it'll all be over.'

She rested her head on my shoulder. 'I'm scared,' she said.

It was not until many months later that I understood what these words meant, and that they had nothing to do with the operation ahead.

Early next morning she lay in bed and watched me dressing. I said I would come up to Liverpool during post-operational leave. This wasn't tempting Fate; I had woken feeling confident that today's mission would be successful. After a pause I added, 'Of course, it won't be the same.'

'It'll never be the same,' she said, and she spoke as though a book had already been closed and was, at this moment, being placed on the shelf of things past.

I finished dressing and said, 'Be seeing you.'

'Take care,' she replied.

13. *Dig's Day*

IT WAS SUNDAY, the 11th March 1945.

Les and I walked to the briefing room. 'It's a funny thing,' he said, 'but Sunday is our lucky day for flying. We fly more on Sundays than on any other day.'

Almost everyone we met called out 'All the best.'

'The whole camp seems to know it's our last flip,' said Les.

We didn't stop at the locker room but went straight to the briefing room. As we reached the door I said, 'Cross your fingers, Les.'

'Aye. Quick, let's have a cigarette.'

We paused and lighted cigarettes.

Inside the briefing room a red ribbon on the wall wound into the heart of the Ruhr. We went closer and saw that the target was Essen.

'Could be worse,' said Les.

We sat at a table and Les began to draw in courses on his Mercator's projection. The briefing room began to fill up. Dig walked in, went to the wall map, turned to look for us, grimaced, and went out. His eyes were red-rimmed, as though he hadn't slept.

Nicky entered and winced when he saw the target was Essen. He came across. 'How do you like it, Mike?'

'All right. How about you?'

He gave a perfunctory oath and went to join his navigator.

Other crew members were allowed in for main briefing.

The Intelligence Officer began. 'This will be the biggest daylight raid by heavy bombers the world has ever seen.'

We had started our tour with a biggest ever daylight raid and were finishing in the same way.

Crews were told that more than a thousand bombers would drop in the region of five thousand tons of bombs. The raid would last half an hour and its object was to wipe out the damaged Krupp's factories and completely dislocate the transport system. The stream would be escorted by two hundred Spitfires and Mustangs. The attack would be controlled by a Master Bomber and since cloud was anticipated blue marker flares would be used. In the event of no flares being visible, and subject to contrary orders by the Master Bomber, bombing should be on GH and flares be released for the following aircraft. H-Hour over the target for the first aircraft was 1500 hours. Our squadron would be near the end of the attack and bomb at H-Hour plus twenty-five.

After the specialized briefings by section leaders the Vicar came forward. 'Well, chaps, the honour of leading the squadron falls to Flight Lieutenant Klenner's crew. This is their last operation and with it they achieve the distinction of being the first crew in the Group ever to complete forty trips on a first tour.' There was a flutter of handclapping. 'I'm sure we all wish them the best of luck,' the Vicar went on, 'and, chaps, let there not be an Essen when you return.' He was about to leave the platform when he remembered something. 'By the way, there will be some big-wigs from Group here this afternoon, so put on a good show when you come back.'

This information was received with a baying howl.

A crew bus took us to K-King's dispersal. '2 TO GO' showed white on the camouflaged brown-green fuselage. Paul began to wipe off the number so that he could replace it with '1.' 'Rub the lot off,' said Dig. 'I never liked it there in the first place.'

Jock and all Able's ground crew, as well as King's ground crew, were present. Perspex had been polished until it gleamed and the guns were loaded ready for use.

Dig called Jock and his men into a small circle. 'Tonight,' he said, 'we all go out and get pissed. It's on us.' The ground crew gave approving murmurs. 'If any of you are standing by closing time,' said Dig, 'I'll want to know why.'

A staff car drove up and the Vicar and Group Captain alighted. They stood making conversation with us until it was time to climb aboard and then they wished us good luck.

As K-King taxied out Dig played with the throttles. 'I'll know how to handle you today, you beaut,' he said.

At the beginning of the take-off he pushed the two port throttles well forward and then inched the starboard throttles up the box. King went straight and true down the runway.

At the point where the stream crossed the battle-lines it might have looked from below as though it was making for a target in north-east Germany but suddenly it veered to the south-east and began the run-in on Essen.

Flak began to spurt up through the cloud but I felt completely at ease; it was as comfortable in my compartment as in an armchair at home.

The Master Bomber was not on the air but blue flares were floating down ahead. Les called up that GH was unserviceable and it was up to me to bomb on the markers.

'I've always been told to take the farthest marker upwind,' I said to Dig with an air of enthusiasm. 'Shall I take it?'

'Take any bloody marker,' he said. 'Get rid of 'em.'

I picked out a marker, gave corrections, and as the spot of burning blue floated into the pale orange graticule I pressed the release. Thirteen thousand pounds of bombs ripped away and as the Cookie left the aircraft lifted.

No hang-ups. 'Close bomb doors, Dig.'

'Roger,' he shouted.

Then the impossible happened. From the mêlée of Lancasters our squadron began formating on King's tail. It was the first time we had ever flown back in formation.

Once past the battle-lines the other pilots switched on the R/T and congratulations came through.

All the way home the squadron flew behind K-King in perfect formation of vics of three. Dig called over the R/T, 'Roughedge from Roughedge aircraft. Aerodrome 1500.'

The reply came not from a WAAF in control but the Vicar. 'Well done, K-King,' he said. Then a girl's voice spoke. 'Roughedge King prepare to land.'

'King preparing to land,' said Dig.

The aircraft on our tail peeled off to port and starboard but King continued straight on before beginning a gentle curve to port and on to the downwind leg.

For the last time Dig and Ray went through their landing drill, repeating to each other stereotyped phrases which were always good to hear, but particularly significant today. Wheels down, half flap, into the funnels, full flap, 2850. As he came in towards the airfield runway Dig deliberately undershot and King roared across the countryside at a height of about fifty feet. He wanted to come in as close as possible to Able's dispersal which lay at the near end of the runway. On the dispersal, waving and dancing, we could see Jock and his boys. The warmth of their greeting was very moving.

King's wheels touched the runway. Ray pulled the throttles back hard. The aircraft slowed to a halt. 'Good show,' said Les quietly and no one else spoke.

As we taxied back to dispersal various airmen waved. At dispersal Dig and Ray cut the engines one by one and there was silence. A crew bus was waiting. 'The Vicar's really looking after us,' said George.

Kit was thrown carelessly into the bus, the driver slammed the doors and ran to his seat. He had orders to bring us to the interrogation room as quickly as possible.

No one said much on that short journey. We sat on two bench seats facing each other. I was opposite Dig. His hat was tipped back on his head and I have never seen a man look so happy. He gazed at each of us in turn as though fixing this moment for ever in his memory. He didn't speak, but he grinned until his cheeks must have ached.

On alighting we learned why we had been rushed back. Not only were senior officers from Group present, but a horde of newspaper reporters and photographers were gathered around.

The Vicar bustled like a hen. 'Interviews after interrogation,' he said to the Press.

A few minutes later we were facing the reporters and Dig no longer looked so happy. In reply to questions he spoke as though each word was an unreliable emissary who might turn and spit in his face. From time to time he attempted to palm off the reporters' questions on to Les and me, but it wasn't our story they wanted. After a series of questions that were as leading as guide dogs the reporters released Dig and we went to be photographed.

.   .   .   .   .

I telephoned Audrey who said, 'Wonderful! Come over as soon as you can.'

I told her that I had promised to celebrate with the crew and Able's ground crew.

'But I thought...,' she began, and then silence descended.

I said I was sorry and would see her when the celebration was over, but as I spoke I felt that my words were hurting her and this made me unhappy because although my loyalties were divided my emotions weren't. I loved her.

My best blue, unworn for months, had verdigris on its buttons. After polishing I went down to the Mess for a drink. Nicky was there sitting by the fire and nursing a pint of beer. He didn't say 'Congratulations' or anything like that; it was 'Coming back for a second tour, Mike?'

I said that of course I was, and he nodded approval. Neither of us could visualize a life without flying.

In the village pub Dig bought the first round, Les bought the second, I bought the third, and then I lost count. We toasted Les, as well as the ground crew, because today was his twenty-third birthday.

I can remember Dig saying that we probably shouldn't get in another tour over Europe, but would we be willing to be his crew on a tour over Japan? We said we would. And everyone swore that, come what may, we would all keep in touch with each other for the rest of our lives.

Audrey returned to Liverpool and the crew went on leave. Dig and Harry came to Ganwick Corner for a short while and, so far as my parents were concerned, nothing was too good for them. Months of carefully hoarded butter and other food was squandered in a few meals.

On one occasion my father said to Dig, 'There must have been times when you were pretty worried.'

Dig thought for a moment. 'Yes, there were,' he said. 'On our last trip in Able I felt worried and tense and then old Mike said something about getting a haircut when we got back, and everything was more settled after that.'

Before we had ever flown together Dig had announced that he had the best crew in Bomber Command and now that the tour was finished he was saying exactly the same thing. As for me, the proof that had been sought had been obtained. I had no idea that it was a proof which in time would demand reproving.

During our leave the Allies bridged the Rhine and spread like a forest fire through Germany. The squadron was grounded for much of the time because no sooner were crews briefed for a target than it was captured and occupied.

On returning from leave we learned that the Order directing crews to fly a first tour of forty operations had been rescinded shortly after we had completed our last trip. The figure was back to thirty. We had, it seemed, been uniquely privileged to be the only crew on the squadron, and probably in the Group, to have completed a first tour of forty ops.

Then Harry, George and I were posted to Catterick for appraisal interviews. From there Harry was sent on indefinite leave, George was sent on a course for Signals instructors and I was posted to an airfield in Anglesey to await a vacancy in a course for bombing instructors. I was still waiting when the news came through that Germany had surrendered and the war in Europe was over.

Squadron crews now flew on mercy missions to bring back prisoners of war, and they also took parties from the ground staff to show them the devastation of Germany's major cities. Then peace came throughout the world. Almost at once the squadron was disbanded and someone, sensing that past was past, and there was no point in keeping records of raids flown or crews briefed, made a bonfire of the squadron's records. It was a time for looking towards the future, and there seemed no point in keeping what were nothing more than souvenirs of what was probably to be the last world war.

Men were posted to different stations all over the country and the aircraft dispersed.

I heard from someone that Dig had been awarded the Distinguished Flying Cross and George and Les had each been awarded the Distinguished Flying Medal.

Nine months after we completed our tour A-Able was sent to the scrap heap. By this time Dig had returned to Australia, the crew had completely disintegrated, and nobody thought of suggesting a reunion.

Occasionally there were chance encounters with men one had known on the squadron and one day I saw an airman I knew by sight. I stopped him in the street, we talked for a few moments, and I asked whether he had any news of Nicky. At first he couldn't remember who Nicky was but after I had given a description an expression of recollection came to the airman's face. 'I know who you mean,' he said.

He then told me that Nicky and all his crew had been on the last operational sortie flown by the squadron. Their aircraft had lost power shortly after take-off, its wing had dipped, and it had crashed. Everyone on board had been killed instantly.[18]

PART TWO

A WIND FROM THE PAST

1. *The Search Begins*

IN CREATING A WIND from the past to blow into the present lives of six men I realized that memories better forgotten might be stirred up. The others might now glance back with a sentimental eye, and by charging into their nostalgia I could emerge as a bull with wisps of dreams hanging from its horns. I was not worried that what had been written could form the basis of a libel action, but there are things published daily which fall short of libel and yet cause distress.

But I wanted to know how they had fared, and to ask the questions mentioned in the Introduction. Of course no theories could be proved by collating their viewpoints on such subjects as fear, and the bombing of Dresden, but it might be possible to draw some general conclusions. And I wondered whether, with the ever-present threat of nuclear holocaust and with race riots and civil disturbances everywhere, they thought our efforts, and the efforts of thousands like us, had been worth while. Or had our youth been as futile as an anonymous postcard addressed to nowhere and dropped unstamped into a disused letter-box.

By chance the first man to appear was not in the crew and was found by Mike Garbett, the project engineer from Birmingham. He discovered the whereabouts of Harry Warwick, the pilot who had ditched C-Charlie during the Witten raid. Warwick was living only a few miles from me. Over the telephone we arranged to meet, with our wives, on the following night.

When he walked into the saloon bar of an hotel on the Barnet by-pass mutual recognition was immediate, and this was surprising since we had flown together only once. He had aged undramatically; his eyes and movements remained alert, and he had the air of self-assurance which gives its owner an aura of solid calm almost as tangible as the body it surrounds and seems to come as part of the kit of all professional pilots. Harry Warwick had continued flying after the war and was employed by a company which makes aerial surveys all over the world. We introduced our wives and then neglected them to reminisce about life on the squadron. He asked almost at once where Dig was, and seemed disappointed that I hadn't heard of him for twenty-three years. I asked him some of the questions I hoped to ask the crew but he had not taken part in the Dresden raid and although he had been through one rather bad period he couldn't attribute this to wartime flying. Indeed, he was grateful for the opportunities the war had provided. As a boy he had always wanted to fly and how else, he asked, could he have afforded to learn this craft? I said that on his one trip with us to Ostafeld I had been impressed by his keenness, and his wife looked quickly at him and smiled.

'We were first off the deck for our first raid as a crew,' he said with pride.

'That was Witten. What exactly happened when you had to ditch?'

His wife leaned forward. 'I should be interested to hear this,' she said. 'He never talks about it.'

He took up the story from when we had last seen C-Charlie fading in the distance, oil bleeding from a damaged engine, escorted by a Mustang, and although we were sitting in a busy hotel bar the impression of a damaged Lancaster limping home was so vivid that our surroundings faded and the only reality was the need to reach the coast of England and safety.

He had been forced to cut two more engines and by the time he descended into cloud over the Channel three engines were dead and he was flying on the single remaining engine. The Mustang pilot, his own fuel reserves dangerously low, had radioed Warwick's position over VHF and then made for his own base. Most of the instruments on the pilot's panel had failed and he was obliged to come down through a blanket of cloud without the aid of an artificial horizon. This, although he didn't say so, is a feat comparable to hurrying blindfold down a strange set of stairs without a banister rail.

Eventually C-Charlie broke the cloud and Warwick saw that he was skimming the sea. Having had no idea of his altitude this came as a nasty shock. He immediately told his crew to take up ditching positions and put the Lancaster down on the water. A heavy sea was running and on impact the aircraft broke in half, but the crew managed to float and scramble on to a dinghy. For four hours they shivered, miserably seasick, in wet clothes and then, with only a vestige of winter daylight left, they were located by a Naval vessel. The dinghy was lashed to the side of the ship and the crew helped aboard. They were given cups of hot cocoa and told that their position was forty miles south-east of Felixstowe.

Their rescuers were cock-a-hoop; not only had seven lives been saved but the Navy was one up in the friendly rescue duel between itself and R.A.F. Air Sea Rescue.

But individual tragedies had only been deferred. A few weeks later Warwick's bomb-aimer fell while jumping off a station bus, the driver didn't apply the brakes, the bus slid back and pinned the fallen man under its wheels. He died almost instantly. Then, shortly after the war, the mid-upper gunner died of cancer. The only other member with whom Warwick had remained in touch was the navigator, and he had continued to serve in the R.A.F. He had reached the rank of squadron leader when he had been killed in a helicopter crash.

A brief silence fell, and then Warwick glanced at his wife. 'We were given a fortnight's leave after Witten and I thought "If this is what ops are like the sooner I get married the better"...We got married before the end of my leave.'

I am sure that Harry Warwick's answers to my questions would have been much the same if we had been drinking alone, but nevertheless I decided that if and when I began to interview the crew it would be without the presence of third parties. Everyone, except the hidebound egotist, suits his conversation to his company and it would be difficult enough to get past the blur of imperfect memory without allowing for the filter of wives and, perhaps, children.

1. George Bell

George was a native of Yeadon in Yorkshire and I had heard from someone (in 1945 I think) that he intended to join the police force after demobilization. I rang directory inquiries for the number of Yeadon police station.

When the final connection was made a policeman gave his name briskly and waited. I said that I was a wartime friend of someone called George Bell who had won the D.F.M. and might possibly at some time have been stationed at Yeadon. 'Hold on just a minute, sir,' the policeman said.

A few moments later he came on the line again to say that a constable George Bell had indeed been at Yeadon many years ago and it was possible that he might now be attached to Doncaster (West Riding) Headquarters. Obligingly he supplied the number and, although it was half-way through the evening, I rang Doncaster.

Luck – it would be arrogant to attribute the good fortune to God, and Fate is for orientals and lovers – was with me and after a short delay I was told that George Bell D.F.M. was at present on a course at the police college at Bramshill House near Basingstoke. Pushing my luck I asked for, and was given, George Bell's private address.

On the following morning I wrote to him. No reply came within a fortnight and so I wrote again, a terse letter which enclosed the following with a request to delete as appropriate:

I am   }   the George Bell D.F.M. who flew with F1.
                  }   Lieut. George Frederick Klenner during the
I am not   }   1939-45 war.

A reply arrived within a week. After apologizing for the delay – he had been moving house and redecorating – he wrote, 'What a wonderful surprise after all these years to hear from you again...I am now an Inspector on a six-month course at the Police College...I wonder if you would like to come to the College one Thursday evening to dinner, we have a formal dinner one evening each week...I saw Paul about 1948-9 but have not heard from him since, he was working in a market in Liverpool at the time. I wrote to Dig two or three times but received no reply. His last address was 174 Jervois Street, Torrensville, Adelaide...No news of any of the others...'

2. Les Walker

The telephone directory showed that an 'L. A. Walker' lived in Sheffield. I rang the number and was told that Mr Walker had moved from that address but could be contacted at another Sheffield number. 'It's a business number,' I was told, 'you'll have to ring him in the morning.'

When I put through a call the next day a man answered.

'Mr Les Walker?' I asked.

'Yes.' The tone was guarded.

'This is a voice from the past. Does the name "Mike" mean anything to you?'

'Mike Tripp!...While you were talking I recognized your voice!'

I explained that I was trying to trace the crew.

'I've sometimes thought about you,' he said. 'When I've seen pop groups on TV. You were born before your time.'

I asked what he was doing.

He hesitated. 'I did a silly thing about five years ago. I bought a grocer's shop.'

To his question, I told him I was a solicitor, on the legal staff of the Charity Commission, and that I wrote novels.

'Your mother should be proud of you,' he said.

'Not really,' I began, and then reverted nearly a quarter of a century, groping for the right words to communicate. To a nearer acquaintance I would have said, 'She doesn't like the bits about sex,' but to Les I found myself saying, 'My books are too near the knuckle for her.'

'I can believe that,' he said. 'You were always,' and his voice faded.

I asked if he had kept in touch with the others.

'No. I lost touch completely after it all finished.'

I told him about the book I was working on and asked, if a reunion could be arranged, whether he would be able to come.

'It might be difficult,' he said. 'The shop.'

Before ringing off I said he would be hearing from me again.

Absurdly I had expected him to jump at the idea of a reunion and when he had begun to talk of his commitments to a shop I had been disappointed. But why should he want a reunion? Most people know the past can only be given a stale breath of life by the repetition of old anecdotes, and that those who devote all their attention to the past are simply walking backwards into their own graves.

3. George 'Dig' Klenner

Over the years I had hopefully asked a number of Australians whether they came from Adelaide but nearly everyone seemed to be a native of Sydney. The only self-confessed Adelaide man (himself an ex-bomber pilot) said there was a fairly large settlement of old European *émigrés* in one part of the town and promised when he returned to try and look up Dig. It was an idle promise.

Mike Garbett wrote that he was attempting to trace Dig through 'Australian contacts' and I decided to send a letter to the occupier of the address George had given me. It was a letter intended to appeal to instincts of goodwill and to reinforce these instincts, I enclosed ten shillings to cover the cost of a reply, even if that reply was simply 'not known at this address'. The letter was never returned as undelivered and presumably the recipient treated the ten shillings as a windfall from a fool with more money than sense, which it undoubtedly was. For the time being, the trail to Dig was cold.

4. Paul Songest

I had not seen Paul since April 1945, and had heard from him only three times since, when in September 1952, he came to stay for the week-end with Audrey and me at our home in Rutland. He had read *Faith is a Windsock*, a first novel about an aircrew, and wanted to see me again.

In the book I had made 'Paul' a hard-drinking mid-upper gunner and was apprehensive lest he might object to this portrait. Far from it, he had read the novel four times in the space of ten days and he said, 'I wouldn't have minded if you'd put the "Songest" in too. I wouldn't have sued for libel.'

He had changed very little although perhaps he was slightly steadied by marriage and two children, the younger of whom he called 'Mike'. He asked Audrey if I had found it difficult to settle down after the war. Never one to waste words when it came to a hard truth she had replied, 'Yes.'

'So did I,' he said, and he told us that he had spent a year gambling on horse and dog races. One day, however, he had become bored with punting, and had gone to his fiancée and said, 'How about December the twentieth for our wedding?' She, like Audrey, came from the north-west of England and was only a little more prodigal in her reply. 'All right,' she had said.

Since that time he had been the manager of a small business in the fish market. 'It's not a bad life,' he had said, 'you work from seven in the morning till one, six days a week, but the rest of the time's your own. I haven't taken a holiday since I started. Life's one long holiday.'

At that time we were living in a village which was near an aerodrome manned by a Canadian fighter squadron. On the Saturday afternoon Paul and I went to a carnival organized by the Canadians. He liked the rolling green countryside and the houses built of Cotswold stone and roofed with Collyweston slates. 'I suppose you're used to it,' he said, 'but it looks pretty marvellous to me after Liverpool.'

Then he asked if I would like to fly on ops again. I said I shouldn't, and he seemed slightly disappointed in me. 'I sometimes wish I could do a couple more,' he said. 'Just for the fun and excitement of it.'

The carnival with its mixture of Rutland villagers and Canadian servicemen with their wives was a great success if only because chocolate, still rationed in England, was freely on sale, and there were stalls selling hot dogs and hamburgers − a taste which had yet to be commercially exploited in England. We watched the square dancing, a band of pipers and some cowboy turns. Paul seemed to enjoy every minute.

In the evening he told us that for some time after the war he had suffered from stomach pains and his doctor, suspecting ulcers, had placed him on a fish and milk diet. One day Paul had decided that he might as well be dead as 'eat this stuff' and he went back to square meals and hard drinking. His stomach had seldom troubled him since. 'It was a case of mind over matter,' he said cheerfully.

When it was time for bed I said I hoped he would sleep well. 'When I sleep it's a little death,' he replied. And those are the last words of his recorded in my diary. He returned by train to Liverpool the following day, and we agreed to see more of each other, but I didn't see him again and my letters and Christmas cards went unanswered. Audrey and I moved from Rutland to Hertfordshire and eventually I stopped sending cards.

It was sixteen years since the last sight of Paul and I began the search by looking up 'Songest' in the Liverpool telephone directory. One name was given.

The woman who answered my call said that there were no Songests at the house. Mrs Songest, who had lived there before her, was an elderly lady, living on her own, who had moved to the south of England. Her present address was unknown.

I wrote to Paul's former address but the occupier, in reply, said that she had never heard of him. She had been living in the house for four years and the previous occupants had been a Mr and Mrs Adams who had emigrated to Australia.

I then looked up 'Songest' in every telephone directory in the United Kingdom. There were seven. I rang each in turn but none of them were related to Paul, nor had they heard of him.

I made inquiries and found that the fish market had been closed for many years.

It seemed as though Paul was going to be difficult to trace.

5. Ray Parke

I knew Ray had come from a Norfolk village and had a vague idea that 'St Mary' formed part of its name. Three such villages existed fairly near Norwich and I decided that when the weather improved I would drive there and start making local inquiries. A search through telephone directories had been unsuccessful.

6. Harry McCalla

Wartime friendships, born of a necessity for mutual protection and comfort against a common danger, seldom survive the slack safety of peace. When I made my home in the country and Harry remained in London it was inevitable that the ties which existed between us should be quietly unravelled. He had given up an attempt to become a barrister, defeated more by a love of pleasure than lack of capability, and he had begun to live, and live well, by his wits. From time to time I received picture postcards from abroad when he was exploring the diversions of such places as Le Touquet and Monte Carlo. Occasionally a letter arrived. In 1950 he wrote one which began:

Dear Mike,
    In the hope of your practice growing apace and in the desire of having your goodly patronage in a problematic business venture, I send you greeting...

He was establishing a club in London's West End and wished me to be a sponsor. All that was required, he said, was that I should be willing to 'say a good word' on his behalf. The remainder of the letter gave a few vague details of the club and it concluded,

I heard recently that Christmas will be here in a few weeks, but I cannot really profess to knowing anything about it, can you?

I replied that he could count on me to say more than one good word on his behalf.
    Nearly two years passed before I heard from him at any length again and then the letter began:

Dear Mike,
    How are you these days? As usual there is a cause for my writing to you. I have fallen very much by the wayside. Within six months I have had such a tremendous change of fortune that I am now forced to seek employment of sorts...

He had given my name as a reference for a job at the Post Office and naturally, when an official letter came asking for a reference, I willingly gave it. But from this point Harry vanished from my life. He didn't answer my letters and in the end I stopped writing.
    Nine years passed and I had given up hope of seeing him again when he telephoned. By this time I was living near Potters Bar; he had obtained my number from my mother who was still living at Ganwick Corner.
    It wasn't an easy conversation. I was thrown when he called me 'sir' not from servility but out of a desire to be formally polite. He

said that he had been married for five years; there were no children. He now worked in the control room of Willesden power station. .

A week later we met for a meal in London and had lunch at a Chinese restaurant in Wardour Street. From notes made shortly after the meeting it is clear that I went to meet him with a sort of pleasurable trepidation, half expecting to find a man who was prideful and arrogant in his twenties humbled and broken in his forties. But I had hopelessly prejudged the situation. He was in far better shape physically than I, he was far better dressed, and he had lost none of his imperious bearing. Again, as in the past, I was impressed by his charm of demeanour and amused by his rueful humour.

During the meal he said that nine years ago he had reached a stage when he realized that he was losing his sense of values. 'I decided to cut with my past life in the West End,' he said. The severance cost him his friends and since he didn't care for the migrants then coming in from the West Indies, he made no new friends. It was a bleak and best-forgotten period in his life when for two years he had worked in a factory packing steel wool. To the question of why he had not answered my letters he gave an apologetic smile and said that he didn't want to be an embarrassment to a professional man.

He had not returned to Jamaica since joining the R.A.F. and he didn't know when, if ever, he would return. For a while we talked about the crew and how, even before the tour had ended, it had become fragmented into splinter groups when we were off-duty. It was not surprising that everyone had lost touch so quickly. I said I should very much like to see Dig again although, at the time, we seemed to have little in common and frequently got on each other's nerves. Harry laughed. 'You know why that was,' he said. 'Although Dig might not have been as intellectual as you, he was more grown up.'

From this time we continued to meet, sometimes for a meal, sometimes just for a quick drink, and we usually went to a pub in Soho. Harry continued to work as a control engineer in various London power stations and, after tracing George and Les, I rang and asked him to meet me.

2. *Harry*

WHENEVER HARRY and I arrange dates it is invariably 'Same place, usual time' and the place is Piccadilly Circus at the draughty corner between Regent Street and Sherwood Street where a bookstall offers magazines of nude poses and paperback stories 'strictly for adults'. The usual time is 12.30 p.m. and it shows a basic conservatism that not only do we have a rigidly fixed system for meeting but also usually walk the short distance to the Red Lion at the corner of Windmill Street and Archer Street. This is a pub with no fancy gimmicks except for one fruit machine. Men, and a few women, come here to drink time away, rather as though it is a job to be done, and they don't require anything more than essential pub furniture and that they can prop themselves against the bar or sit at one of the tables. At least, this is the lunch-hour pattern. It is a long time since I have been in the Red Lion at night.

I believe it was Louis XIV who said that punctuality is the politeness of princes. Harry, however far he had to travel, always arrived within two minutes of 12.30 and on this cold winter day I was grateful for his punctuality. We walked briskly to the Red Lion and, after getting drinks, we sat at a table and I outlined my plans for a book. Harry listened with absorption and when I asked whether he would answer a few questions, as accurately as possible after such a lapse of time, he said, 'Go ahead.'

'For a start, what made you volunteer for aircrew duties?'

'I had just left school and was in a dull Civil Service job in Kingston.'

'What job?'

'The Collector General department of the Revenue. The R.A.F. seemed exciting and glamorous. My mother didn't like it much but my old man thought it would make a man of me.'

'You were a bit wild?'

'A bit.'

'How old were you?'

'Twenty-two.'

'Do you think the R.A.F. and flying changed your character?'

'It was like going from a small world into a big world. Jamaica was small and narrow. It was more than a renaissance to me — it was a revolution. It had a revolutionary effect on my life.'

'In some ways you are more an Englishman now than a Jamaican.'

'Thank you for saying so.'

'What would you have been if you'd gone back to Jamaica after the war?'

'I would probably have ended up like my old man. He was a marine pilot...But certainly war changed things for me. Everything was so *new*!'

'How about fear? Were you afraid very often?'

'Fear never entered into it at gunnery school. It was all fun. But there were a few occasions later.'

'When?'

'The first time flak burst right under the tail. And another time was after the second overshoot at St Eval. Were there two or three overshoots?'

'Three.'

'This was the second overshoot. I was afraid then. The engines were red hot.'

'Did flying leave you with any physical or mental disability?'

'No.'

'But you had a bad stomach for years. I remember you couldn't drink half a pint of beer without stomach pains.'

'That's true, but it wasn't the flying. Those meals we had. Except for the flying meals it was spam and potatoes.'

'What about mental disability?'

Harry hesitated, and when he spoke it seemed to be at a tangent and tortuously expressed. It occurred to me that he was talking about the difficulties of being a coloured man in England.

'You mean this so-called colour question?'

'It was all right until the English became aware of colour.'

'When was that?'

'About 1955 or 1956, I'd say. I had difficulty in getting a flat then. There were so many immigrants coming in. Uneducated people... They are labourers, but not like English labourers. There is no equivalent in England. And they don't know how to keep themselves to themselves. I have never yet lived in a flat where they are among the other tenants. And if I, a coloured man, don't want their company, why should the English be expected to want their company?'

'After the war you had a fracas with a bus conductor?'

Harry fingered a scar beneath his right eye. 'Yes, but that wasn't colour. I got on the bus and he came racing up the stairs on my heels shouting "Fares please". I said, "Give us a chance". He said something that got up my nose and I called him an ignorant bastard. Then he hit my face with his ticket rack.'

He told me that the police had brought proceedings against the conductor who was found guilty and fined. The magistrate had advised Harry that he could sue in a civil court for damages, but he had taken no action. 'The man had a wife and kids to support,' he explained.

'Do you look back on them as good times or bad?'

'The greatest years of my life. The most wonderful.'

'Have you got any special memories?'

'Only that time in J-Jig. You remember? When we crashed and I was on a charge for not being in the tail.'

'What do you recall as the worst raid?'

He thought for a while. 'The time I saw two Lancasters behind us being blown up by bombs dropped from aircraft above them. Paul saw more than two, I think, because he said, "There goes another, Harry" but you'd have to ask him.'

'I wish I could. I don't know where he is.'

'That was the worst raid.'

'It was the second Solingen raid.'

'Was it? I don't remember.'

'What about the time you had frostbite?'

'There was ice all over my oxygen mask and frost over my helmet. I remember showing Paul the ice and knocking it off before we got out of the aircraft.'

'Do you remember the time you took a stand because a West

Indian airman had been sentenced to seven days jankers?'

'Not the details, but I still have the letter from the M.P. somewhere.'

(My father had written to his Member of Parliament expressing concern at the treatment Harry had received.)

'The M.P.'s name was J. Bartle Bull,' Harry continued. 'He wrote saying he'd taken it up with Air Ministry and they replied that the Flight Sergeant was not reprimanded for trying to help his fellow countryman but for the way he went about it.'

'Why do you think we disbanded so easily?'

'Well, we didn't have much in common, did we?...Something else I have just remembered. That time you were playing the piano in the Mess and I got two plates of sandwiches for us. I'd just brought them across when a new man, a sergeant with 'South Africa' on his sleeve, came across and took all the sandwiches off one plate. I asked what he thought he was doing and he said, "*You* don't speak to me like that. I'm a South African." I went for him and he ran away. You chased us both and caught me at the entrance to the Mess. You told me to watch it or, with that other business on my hands, I'd end up by being court martialled.'

'I can remember some trouble with a South African but I can't remember the details...Harry, do you get any intuitions these days?'

'Hardly ever. I used to when I was younger.'

'That Chemnitz affair. It was incredible.'

'I don't know. I did geography at school. European names were familiar to me.'

'But to get Chemnitz like that.'

'Well, I think that perhaps I — my race — are nearer to the beginnings than yours.'

'You mean that white man has lost some of his powers with civilization. At one time he had more than five senses?'

'Yes, I think so.'

'I've often wondered whether it was some sort of telepathy between us. I very much wanted you to pick the right place. What do you think?'

'I think that's very likely. It could have been telepathy.'

'No scientist would ever believe that. It couldn't be proved.'

'No.'

'But you think there are other communications besides words?'

At this point our conversation veered away from flying reminiscences to extra-sensory perception, but later I asked whether he had any memories of Dresden and any views about its destruction.

'No special memories,' he said.

'Was it simply a raid like any other?'

'Yes. Except for the length of time. Was that the longest or was it Chemnitz?'

'Dresden was the longest. You had no qualms that we were bombing refugees?'

Harry shook his head.

'There's one last thing I want to ask you. I know that subjectively you think our tour was worth while, but how about objectively? With the world as it is today, was it all worth it?'

'Worth it,' he exclaimed. 'Of course it was. No question of it. It would have been ten times worse today if Britain had lost the war.'

And then he began to talk of politics. Harry, more than any of us, had always been interested in political theories and ideological clashes, but perhaps he was most passionately concerned with individual rights and liberties. He was for individual freedom and against authoritarian control whether the control emanated from an R.A.F. Group Captain or a Socialist government. A man, he asserted, should be free to speak his piece whether it was on behalf of an ignorant fellow countryman or whether it was against the integration of these same countrymen into English society. For Harry, freedom of speech was a transcendental freedom.

3. *George*

THE CAR HEADLIGHTS picked out an avenue of tall winter-bare trees which disappeared in endless duplication as the road ahead dipped and rose. In the far distance lights twinkled at the top of a hill. Eventually the car passed a keep, went over a bridge and the trees disappeared. I drove into a courtyard where other cars were parked in front of a massive brick-built country house which had a magnificent porch and loggia with three arches. Above the central arch was a fine semi-circular oriel.

I picked up my papers and climbed out of the car. A voice called, 'No need to lock up here,' and I saw a man in evening dress standing on the wide steps of the main entrance. The lights were behind him but I recognized George.

He took my coat and papers and after leaving them in a reception room led me to the bar. It was crowded with men in evening dress and there were a few women wearing long evening dresses and jewels which matched the sparkle in their eyes. The bar was in a lofty panelled room and George told me that Bramshill House had once been a stately home. It had been largely built in the early part of the seventeenth century and tapestries designed by Rubens hung on the walls of an adjoining room.

He had a whisky and dry ginger and I ordered a gin and tonic. We seemed to laugh and grin a lot but although this may partly have been due to nervousness, much was a genuine pleasure at meeting again. He asked about the others in the crew. I said that I had yet to meet Les, but neither Dig, Paul nor Ray had yet been traced.

After a couple of drinks we went into a long banqueting hall for dinner. There must have been about two hundred and fifty people present and the place was brilliantly illuminated because a film unit was making a documentary police film about the function. George introduced me to a number of men at our table, mostly in their late thirties, and we stood until the guests of honour arrived. When they came they walked self-consciously with a camera back-tracking ahead of them.

The grace was brief — 'For good food and good fellowship, thank God' — and we sat down. George poured two glasses of white wine from a bottle which stood in front of our places.

His first reminiscence was of something I had not only forgotten but was unable to recall even after he told me. He was incredulous. 'You don't remember when I got stuck to the Elsan?'

I said I didn't.

'I stood up and it came up with me. I think it was frozen to me. Then it spilled. We agreed to say that the mess was a result of having to take violent evasive action.'

Nor did I remember his rag doll. He said he took it on every raid together with a brassiere and a pair of knickers. 'Dig wouldn't fly unless I had my doll on board,' he said. 'Don't you remember we turned back once on our way to dispersal because I'd forgotten to bring it?'

We talked easily; there were no awkward moments or uneasy silences, and I found that he had changed as little in outlook as he had physically. He told me that after we had broken up as a crew he had been posted to a station near Plymouth on flying control duties. Two months after demobilization he had joined the police force and from then on his life had been slogging, steady, sheer hard work, gradually obtaining promotion until his breakthrough last year to the rank of inspector. He was still married to Rose and his son was twenty-two years old and also married. He had no other children.

His first flight since the war had taken place five years ago when he had been sent on a police air observers' course. He said that he had been scared at first because Dig wasn't at the controls. It had been because he had not wished to fly with anyone else that he had turned down the opportunity of a commission in the R.A.F. 'The only commissions,' he explained, 'were flying commissions.'

After the meal we went to a reception room where there was a bar; we bought whiskies and sat at a table. I asked if flying had changed his nature or character in any way.

He thought before replying and said, 'When you've finished you've seen so many people go down. So many friends lost. It makes you grow up. You become a man before you were a boy. And there was companionship. Wonderful comradeship.'

'It was this sense of belonging to a team which attracted you to the police, I expect?'

'Definitely.'

He said he had often been afraid.

'It was a sort of elated fright. You didn't feel a thing until almost to the target. You saw all the flak. All the explosions around. You stood in the astrodome and you felt all excitement. You thought the man next door was going down but not you. I would have a look, go back and sit down, then get up and have another look. I had such confidence in Dig. A brilliant pilot.'

I said that the war didn't seem to have left him with any disabilities, and I mentioned Paul's ulcers and the bad stomach which Harry attributed to spam and potatoes.

'I had an ulcer that burst last year,' he said. 'I nearly died and was only saved by blood transfusions in the ambulance.'

But he didn't know the cause of the ulcer. It could have been due to 'the variants of police work'.

I asked how it all seemed in retrospect.

'You forget the bad times,' he said. 'You only remember the times when it was scrubbed and a great cheer went up, and you went down to the pub for a drink...Do you remember the rum we used to get out of tin mugs at interrogation?'

'Any special memories, George?'

'That crash in the Stirling is the most vivid. That and the Witten raid. I was in the astrodome and saw the Lanc just behind our tail to the port when it was hit. It blew up. A great ball of fire. Smoke. A ball of flame.'

'How do you account for the crew's easy disbanding?'

'I've often wondered about that, Mike. I can't explain it. One minute we were all together, the next minute it was all gone. I think we parted without realizing we were finished. And we'd always spoken about having reunions, but we never did. You don't know what a thrill it was when I got your letter.'

'I think we were all getting a bit fed up. We'd been too close for too long.'

'Maybe. I can't understand why Dig never wrote. I wrote to him.'

'I remember you — perhaps you won't agree — but I remember you as being up in the clouds one minute and depressed soon after. You seemed to fluctuate, but perhaps I'm wrong.'

'No. I know what you mean. It was when Dig began to see less of us. He was commissioned and had to stay with his own sort. That was only right. But I felt we were drifting apart. He put on sergeant's uniform and came down to our Mess, but it wasn't the same. We saw less and less of him. I liked it best when we were all together. In the end, when he was made flight commander, we hardly saw him off duty.'

To my question about Dresden he said he couldn't remember the briefing and that we had been told of refugees in the city. He had no recollection of the raid and had no feelings of guilt for having taken part in it. When you were fighting a war, you were fighting a war. Mistakes were made but that was war. It is easy in peacetime, and with hindsight, to see what could have been done better or what should have been left undone.

The ambit of our conversation grew wider. Before I left, he gave a warm invitation for a return visit on the following month and asked me to bring Audrey along. In turn, he would ask his wife to come. We had been together four and a half hours when I collected my papers and went outside.

I was wearing an overcoat but George stood shivering in evening dress as I scraped frost from the car's windscreen. I told him to go back into the warm. 'No, I'll stay,' he said. He could have added, but didn't, 'I know my duties as a host as well as I know my police duties.' And I could have said, but didn't, 'It's like you to show crew solidarity by standing out here in the cold.'

When the windscreen was clear I climbed into the car and started the engine. By now George had to clench his jaw to prevent his teeth chattering, but he remained, standing his ground and waving, until I had driven out of his line of vision.

A few weeks later he wrote:

Dear Mike,
    Thank you very much for a sight of the draft. I enjoyed reading it very much and it brought back memories...I never

realized that the differences were so marked between us. I suppose the good things are easily remembered and the not so good ones are pushed right back in the mind and forgotten. I can only say — thank God I joined the crew that I did. I couldn't have found a better...

4. *Les*

HE WAS STANDING by the ticket barrier at Sheffield Midland station. It was late on a cold grey February afternoon and he was wearing a short grey overcoat. I recognized his stance rather than his face; he was looking older than I had expected and his hair had receded; but there was no doubt of the warmth of his welcome. His blue eyes flickered shyly at me before he politely looked away. He had no doubt registered that I was looking much older too, and my hair was grey turning to white.

We drove in a Ford Anglia estate car to his bungalow seven miles away at Dronfield Woodhouse. It was a modern building on the fringe of an extensive housing development and from one window there was a view across soft green Derbyshire hills. I was introduced to his son who was eighteen and studying to be a surveyor. Les had no other children.

We didn't talk about flying or the old times; I had the feeling it would be better to ease gently into this subject rather than rush in with an eager interrogation. Les had been the most reticent man in the crew, but when I was young I had often equated reticence with insensitivity, and this was a measure of my own insensitivity. I learned that he was working for Sheffield Corporation in a job concerned with the financing of building projects. His wife ran a grocery store, and because she would not be home until after eight he prepared the dinner.

It wasn't until we were sitting down to the meal that I asked whether he remembered much about the Dresden raid, and whether he had followed the controversy which had resulted from the publication of *The Destruction of Dresden* by David Irving.

'I did see something on television about it,' he said, 'but I don't remember what.'

I outlined the main debating points.

'I remember the briefing,' he said, 'or rather, how it began. I shall never forget that. The Intelligence Officer said, "Dresden is noted for its silk stockings and the Russians are seventy miles away from it."...I remember that because I always thought Dresden was famous for its porcelain.'

'Did you have any misgivings that we were bombing it, or that we bombed Chemnitz the following night?'

Les thought for a few moments. 'No, I didn't have any misgivings,' he said. 'War is war. They hit you, and you hit them back.'

'Do you remember anything special about the raid?'

'Only over the target. I had a quick look. I remember there were white vapour trails in the red sky. I remember seeing that.'

We were half-way through the meal and Les suddenly seemed more relaxed, and the rather wicked grin I had seen many times spread across his face. 'Do you remember that time we came down through cloud and found we were over the Thames estuary? We should have been over the Naze. We were low and saw a fort. We fired off the colours of the day to stop them shooting at us.'

I said I didn't remember this incident at all.

'I do,' he said, 'we were right off course.' And he gave a chuckle. His wife and son were eating unobtrusively and made no attempt to join the conversation. I decided to abandon the rigid plan not to ask questions in front of third parties; Les seemed to be warming to reminiscence. I began to talk of Harry's intuitions.

Les nodded. 'I shan't forget it,' he said, 'when a trip to Hamburg was cancelled Harry said that if it had been on he wouldn't have flown.' He gave a laugh. 'Do you remember those doughnuts the Church Army canteen used to sell? I don't usually like doughnuts but they were the best I've ever tasted in my life.'

I asked what raid was the worst for him.

'The first. Without any doubt.'

'We took ages to catch up with the bomber stream.'

'Aye, and that was my fault.'

I said I hadn't realized this.

'Oh, yes. I set the DR compass wrong and we set off in a completely wrong direction. After that I kept on making mistake after mistake. It was sheer panic. Nerves.'

'We caught up in the end.'

'It was nobody's fault but mine. Everything went wrong on that raid just as everything went right on the next.'

'Were there any other bad raids?'

'No. Only the last.'

I was startled. 'Essen?'

'GH had packed up and I had nothing to do, so I stood behind Dig and looked out. I didn't like it.'

Later, when we had drunk coffee, and his wife was washing up dishes and his son was in bed, I asked why he had volunteered for aircrew.

'It was simply that I didn't like the idea of foot-slogging,' he said with such certainty that there didn't seem anything to add, but after a pause he said, 'I'd been turned down by the Fleet Air Arm so I joined the R.A.F. I didn't want to walk. That was all.'

'Do you think that operational flying changed your nature in any way?'

'I don't think so.'

'What about fear? Were you often afraid?'

'The only occasions I was afraid were when I wasn't working. So long as I was working in my cabin I was all right. I couldn't see out. There was a blanket in the way. Sometimes I could hear a bang when the flak exploded but I kept myself occupied. I was afraid that last trip, like I said, and that time you were sick and we had a spare bomb-aimer. He went round twice and I wasn't occupied on the second run-in. I remember telling him, "Put jettison bars across. Get rid of 'em!" It was only later I learned it was risky to drop bombs on jettison.'

'So your memory of ops is mainly of watching green blips on radar and plotting tracks on a Mercator's?'

'That's right.'

'Did the war affect your job in later life?'

'No, I don't think it did. I should have been a clerk in a builder's office if there hadn't been a war, and anything might have developed from that.'

'Were they good times or bad, Les?'

'Good. I don't remember any times that were bad. Only when my stomach wasn't right. I was airsick all the time until O.T.U. I don't

141

know whether you remember but I never went on fighter affiliation exercises. And, at Feltwell, when we were doing circuits and bumps in Lancs, I had to get out to stop being sick.'

'I don't remember that. I had no idea you were airsick-prone.'

He laughed. 'I certainly was. Luckily I was never sick on ops.'

'Did the war affect your health at all? Paul told me years ago he thought it had given him ulcers, and I have a back complaint that might be due to flying tensed up.'

'I had an ulcer too. My stomach troubled me, even in those days, and it kept troubling me after the war. It was a duodenal. I had it out in 1956. I felt much better after.'

'But no one could prove that flying caused it?'

'I know I couldn't hold my soup steady in my spoon after we finished,' he said. 'My hands shook so. I couldn't get it up to my mouth without spilling it. In the end, I used to drink soup out of a cup.'

'Have you flown since you were demobbed?'

'No.'

'Would it worry you to fly again?'

'No, I don't think so.'

'How do you account for the crew's easy disbanding?'

'Well, we lived, ate and slept, and more or less played together for a year and a half...'

'Not as long as that. Less than a year.'

'Was it? Anyway, we'd had enough. You got to the end. It was broken up. And that was that.'

We continued talking until after midnight. I slept in the spare room and, the following morning, when his wife had gone to the shop and his son had left the house, Les prepared breakfast for us both. He had taken a day's leave from the office.

When we had eaten, I read out what I had written about the briefing for the Dresden raid and asked whether, so far as he remembered it, the account was accurate. He said he thought it was, although his particular memory was the information that Dresden was famous for the manufacture of silk stockings.

He mentioned an incident I had forgotten. He, George, Paul and Ray had been out for the evening and had become very drunk. He had returned to the billet before the others and fallen asleep fully dressed on his bed. When they came in they propped him up so that, still asleep, he was standing to attention on his bed. Then they let go and he fell to the floor and cut and bruised one eye. Early the following day he went to briefing and was told by the navigation leader that he was to be a wind-finder for the day. (It was the practice at this stage in the war for five navigators in the bomber stream to calculate the strength and direction of the wind and for their pilots then to transmit the findings to the leading aircraft on R/T. An average of the five winds would be computed and the stream would be given this wind as the correct prevailing wind.)

The navigation leader after telling Les he was a wind-finder had looked at him closely and said, 'God help the stream if they use your wind.'

In due course, while flying over France, Les had calculated a wind and given it to Dig for transmission. Then, over the R/T they heard the wind of another navigator. It was twenty miles an hour different from Les's and fifteen degrees out. In terms of aerial navigation the discrepancy was disastrous. In some agitation Dig had asked, 'What the hell shall I do, Les? Shall I give them your wind, or shall I simply repeat the one we've just heard?'

Les, suffering from a bad hangover, had said, 'To hell with it. Give 'em mine.'

Dig had, and when the other three winds were provided it was found that Les's wind was closer to the average than any. After landing he had walked towards the interrogation room, his eye still bruised and swollen from falling off the bed, and a WAAF had come running towards him. 'She wanted to know if we'd been hit on the raid,' he said with a laugh.

We talked about WAAFs for a while and he asked if I remembered the WAAF with laughing eyes who was working in the cookhouse. She had been a notorious chop-girl. Every squadron seemed to have a chop-girl. These were the women fated to pick boy-friends who were shortly to be killed. The chop-girl on our squadron was reputed to have lost five boy-friends, killed on operations. It was, of course, nothing more than a series of tragic coincidences for the girls involved, but most flyers are superstitious about such coincidences and the word 'chop-girl' was coined. I remembered the girl, not for her laughing eyes, but because George had danced with her a few times at a station dance. It was ridiculous but until we had flown, and returned safely from the next operation, I was worried lest some supernatural influence working through the medium of a pretty cookhouse WAAF might be stronger than the crew's skills and the other imponderables of survival.

At midday Les drove me to the railway station. I thanked him for his hospitality and said I would let him know any future developments in the search. 'All the best,' he replied.

For some time after leaving him I thought about the quality of courage. In spite of airsickness on every flight he had completed his training, and in spite of fears which kept him hidden in his compartment during most of our tour he had progressed from an indifferent to a first-class navigator. He had done himself less than justice by saying that he had joined the R.A.F. to avoid foot-slogging, and I was aware that never in the past had I been remotely aware of the complexities of human nature which are simply reduced to 'motive' in detective stories and everyday speech. I shall never know what driving forces made Les volunteer for the R.A.F. after having been rejected by the Fleet Air Arm, nor shall I know what made him persist with his training although wretchedly airsick time after time. I shall never understand these things; I can only wonder at the mixture of humility and aggression which is latent in all humanity and which can, balanced one way or the other, lead to Man's salvation or his total destruction.

5. *'Dig'*

DIG AND I had virtually nothing in common except a desire to survive. I was frequently irritated by the repetitive 'You'd whinge if your arse was on fire' and 'It's a great life if you don't weaken' and yet strangely I have carried these sayings into later life and now, in middle-age, sometimes catch myself muttering 'It's a great life if you don't weaken' and if my children haven't heard the word 'whinge' they have heard nothing I have ever said.

The years passed and I found myself thinking of Dig quite often. In particular I remembered an incident late at night at Leighton Buzzard shortly after the crew had been formed. We had all been standing on the pavement and a tough-looking soldier had deliberately selected Paul as a target and walked straight into him. Paul had reeled back and said, 'Look where you're going, mate.' Instantly the soldier squared up for a fight.

He was a stupid man because he was outnumbered six to one, but there was no fight. Dig intervened and calmly said, 'Why did you pick on the smallest of us? Why not pick on me?' The soldier told him to mind his own business. 'I'm asking you a question,' said Dig. 'You want to pick a fight, why not pick a fight with me?'

And so it went on, with Dig growing very scornful of men who tried to pick fights with smaller men, until the soldier, almost bursting with frustration and impotent of vocabulary, began to stalk off.

'On your way,' Dig called contemptuously.

The soldier swaggered back. 'You talking to me?'

'That's right, and I'm telling you to be on your way.'

Again the soldier turned on his heel and walked away. He had been beaten not by muscle, nor by verbal intimidation, nor by rank, but simply by a will stronger than his own.

For me, the years of peace brought into focus and magnified Dig's virtues. He epitomized courage and loyalty, and the incident when he had stepped in to protect Paul was illustrative of both. It was useless to tell myself that Dig was an ordinary human being, fallible, no better and no worse than most people, he became a symbol of the two qualities which, emotionally, I admire the most in mankind...I realize, of course, that at the time of writing (1968) 'guts' is a word so out of fashion as to belong to the age when the wheel was invented, and loyalty is at a discount in every relationship from the rat-race of career-making to the in-fighting of marriage.

The search for Dig had petered out and I found that Mike Garbett had heard nothing from his Australian contacts. Without much hope I went one day to Australia House in the Strand intending to spend a lunch-hour looking through Australian telephone directories. These were kept in the library and I asked the librarian for the directory for South Australia.

The book opened at the section for Adelaide and at the letter 'M.' I turned back to 'K' and ran my finger down the page and found 'Klenner, G. F.' The search had lasted about thirty seconds. Tremendously excited I asked the librarian what the time was in Australia and how much it would cost to telephone. She told me it was 9.30 in the evening and the cost was about a pound per minute.

Within a quarter of an hour I had made a person to person call to the Adelaide number and I heard a woman's voice saying, 'No, he won't be in till midnight.' The operator came back to me, 'Do you wish to book a call for midnight Australia time, 3.30 p.m. in London?' I said, 'Yes, please.'

My telephone rang at exactly 3.30. As I picked it up I decided I wouldn't call him 'Dig' − this name might now be unfamiliar to him and put him at a slight disadvantage − so I said, 'Hello, George.'

'Hello, Mike.'

'How are you?'

'How are you?'

'Fine. And you?'

'I'm fine.'

'Look George,' I began, and I explained that I had an office job in London and also wrote books. 'I'm writing a book about the crew.'

He said something I didn't catch but the relief that he now understood the reason for my call came through clearly.

I told him briefly the news of Harry, George and Les, and asked if there was any possibility of him coming to London.

He laughed. 'I don't think so.'

'Then I'll have to come to Adelaide,' I said on the spur of the moment.

'Damn good idea!'

Trapped by my own enthusiasm I asked about local accommodation.

'We're a bit cramped here,' he said, 'but there's a motel near by.'

'That'll do lovely,' I said, and part of my mind was startled to hear my voice. I wasn't aware that normally I thought ungrammatically and lightning corrections were made before a thought was uttered in speech. I asked what his job was, and was still so surprised at hearing my own 'That'll do lovely' that I missed all of his answer except the words, 'General Motors.'

'Do you fly at all?'

'Not for years.'

'Any children, George?'

'Three.'

I couldn't think of anything else to say.

'Listen George, I've got your address. I'll write and tell you my plans.'

'Okay, Mike. I'll fix things this end.'

'Good. I'll ring off now, but I'll be seeing you.'

'Cheerie-be then for now.'

The line went dead.

For a while I fooled myself that I could easily take-off and fly to Australia, but it became clear that this would need a considerable rearrangement of my time-table. And there were other personal factors to be taken into account. In the end, and with much regret, I deferred the trip and, after apologizing to Dig by letter I asked if he could answer some questions.

I didn't expect a very long letter in reply, and would not have been surprised if no letter had arrived, but he wrote and, because his words are better than any paraphrase of mine his letter is reproduced.

Dear Mike,

It was great to receive your letter even if the opening sentence was most disappointing as we were all looking forward to seeing you...Now to answer the questions for you. This is not easy for me, Mike, as I have always had trouble putting my thoughts on paper so that they read intelligently to others.

What made me volunteer for aircrew duties? I remember telling my father that I was going to join the air force as soon as I turned 18, to which he replied that as they would not call me up until 19 he hoped it would all be over by then. When the time came he did not stand in my way and willingly signed my paper to join, as although he was of German parents who emigrated to Australia about 1885, he was born in this country and was one of the most patriotic men I knew. He served in the Army during the 1914/18 war having joined the day war was declared, his army number was 84, and went through the whole show winning the M.C. in France. We lived in an area which was built for returned servicemen shortly after 1919 and this meant that most of the families were about the same age and in our immediate area of about 20 homes there were 16 boys all within 2 years of being the same age and of these 3 were my closest friends. Of the 16 lads, 15 served overseas and all returned safely. I don't know if I have answered your question exactly, Mike. Dad had always instilled a sense of duty into me by his own actions and I wanted to help in time of trouble.

Did flying change me? I do feel that being in the services, meeting and living with chaps that you would not otherwise have met, the travel overseas, the responsibility, helped me to mature more than I would have otherwise. Prior to the war I lived a very close home life of sport and fun with the other lads and regular fishing trips with my father almost every second week-end from the time I was 10 to the time of joining up. We were more like elder and younger brother than father and son and this is the way we were right up to the time he passed away 6 years ago.

148

I do feel that it changed my outlook on life in that it taught me to live life to the full while you can because death is with us all the time and could claim us at any moment. I guess I feel that having lived through the times that we had I am living on borrowed time. Don't get me wrong, Mike, I am grateful for the life I have had, before during and after the war, and I hope I am spared to see my children grow up and achieve success in their life. But if this is not to be, then I accept it and do not worry about it.

Was I afraid? Yes, I was afraid often. In fact, on all of our ops. A man would have to be stupid or a liar that under those circumstances claimed to be without fear, and I must say that during our tour I had a very strong desire to live although, as you mentioned in your letter, my low flying efforts over East Anglia may not have given this impression.

Mike, I was always very tense after completing an op and this helped to relieve the tensions (letting off steam). I remember one occasion when returning we were flying low over the top of a cloud bank when I let go and threw the tail around by kicking the rudder bars. I got a blast from Harry! Poor guy must have been rattling around like a pea in a barrel back in his turret.

I know that I was always much happier once we settled ourselves in the kite before an op as the waiting for take-off seemed to drag and things were much better with something to concentrate on.

Health. Sorry to hear that Paul, Les and George suffered with ulcers. I can't understand why the spam gave Harry stomach trouble as I quite enjoyed the dish. For myself, I got a very inconvenient disability — deafness — I have lost 60 per cent of my hearing, both ears, and the doctors have attributed this to flying. I have worn a hearing aid for the last 16 years which at the best of times is a damn nuisance. Sorry to hear about your crook back, Mike. Are you sure it was tension?

No, wartime flying did not affect my job as I returned to General Motors Holdens after being discharged and virtually picked up where I left off. We had a reconstruction training scheme for ex-servicemen which permitted us to attend school in the course of our choosing. I trained for my draughtsman's certificate and worked my way up to chief draughtsman in the plant of equipment design section. Since 1962 I have been Project Engineer for our toolroom and this month completed 27 years with the company.

After 23 years I best remember the good times. I think the mind naturally rejects the memories of bad times, and who can remember a short time after it happened just how he felt when he ran into trouble on a trip. It is next to impossible to describe the feelings one felt on any one trip to someone who didn't share it with you.

Special memories? I think the most moving, and yet strangest, occasion was crewing-up. To me this still seems like some strange dream in that over a hundred men sorted themselves into groups of six and that they should learn to live, eat, sleep and fly, and in a lot of cases, die together. How did we get together? I can't remember what was said between each individual member except for Paul and Harry.

When I asked Paul if he would be one of my gunners he said 'Yes' but only if I would take his mate, Harry. I have always admired Paul for this attitude. I have sometimes wondered, although I never asked this while we were together, if Paul had been asked by other pilots and then been rejected because of Harry's colour. To me, Harry is a man I am proud to have known and I vividly remember him bravely marching into the Winco's office to speak on my behalf when I pranged that Stirling.

Remember that last trip? To me that was something special. A thousand-bomber raid, leading the squadron, and coming all the way back to the aerodrome in formation. Then the interviews with the Press and the write-up in the papers. And the evening in the pub. I still can't understand how we got away with taking all that mob, ground crew, WAAFs, and all sorts of bods, back to the sergeant's mess after getting kicked out of the pub.

The worst trip? Dec. 12th 1944, operations daylight to Witten in 'P.' Remember the fighters milling around to port ahead of us? They turned out to be 109s and 190s and they really got into the stream that day. That was the closest we were to other planes that got shot down.

There is another trip that comes to mind, Mike, and on this one you were not with us. We took some poor bomb-aimer on his first trip and on the bombing run he overshot and didn't drop the load. So we stooged around in a circle and let him have another go. I don't mind admitting I wasn't too happy about that, and I've no doubt the other lads weren't particularly pleased either.

Dresden. At the time of the raid I didn't have many thoughts on it at all because it was just another job to be done and I must admit I wasn't fully aware of the situation. It was after learning the damage we did, and it was not really a military target at all, that I felt upset. The subject has been discussed here a few times since the war but only mildly because I haven't met another Aussie who was on the raid. I feel that this raid was laid on at the request of the Russians and was political.

Mike, I hope you can sort out some sense from all this. Don't hesitate to ask for more if it is not quite what you are after.

My best wishes to your family,

As ever,

George.

Dig's letter made me understand why Harry's remark — 'He was more grown up than you' — was true. Dig was more grown up because he had modelled himself on his father and was half-way to being a man before he attained manhood. Although I respected my father we were never like brothers. I grew up more with my mother than with him and the only memory I have of sharing something with him was when he helped me with Latin homework and collecting postage stamps. In many ways he was a kindly man, but he was not always easy to approach, and, in retrospect, I can see I modelled myself on nobody.

I have read in works on psychology about the need for a 'father figure.' I cannot say that consciously I have ever needed such a figure, and it seems unlikely that I ever shall. For a while God was a sort of father figure but the God of my childhood was the God of the Holy Bible, a somewhat terrifying deity in the Old Testament who sailed uneasily through the New Testament wearing a different guise as a God of Love. Eventually I faced God and it was rather like facing fear; God grew less.

Perhaps I am over-sensitive to the father-son relationship because my own son, now twenty-three years old, has for the last ten years been in a mental hospital with a severe form of schizophrenia, and perhaps I am attributing too much of what Dig is to the man who was Dig's father. And yet all the evidence indicates that a sort of chain, or repetitive pattern, is formed between mother and daughter and son and father. The normal child does, quite unconsciously, copy the parent of its own sex in attitudes of mind, prejudices and preferences, taste and moral judgements.

Dig has three children, a girl aged fifteen and boys aged twelve and nine. I would take a bet that his sons will grow as close to him as he was to his own father. But this is no place to elaborate on such a theme. I have only dwelt on it because Ray, when I finally met him, said something which had never occurred to me. He said, 'Of course, Dig was like a father to us.'

6. Ray

OH WHERE OH WHERE HAS RAY PARKE GONE?

THIS WAS A headline to a column in the *Eastern Daily Press* which continued:

> A group of former R.A.F. colleagues are at present making inquiries in Norfolk to try and trace a wartime friend, named Ray Parke, who came from a Norfolk village with the words 'St Mary' in its name...Now one of them is writing a book about their exploits which cannot be finished until the remaining members are traced. The *Eastern Daily Press* learnt of this situation in a phone call from Inspector Russell Browne. While taking a course at police college recently he met another of the former crew, Inspector George Bell, now in the West Riding Police Force...

George had told me of a police friend in Norwich whose help he would try to enlist in tracing Ray and this was one reason why I had delayed visiting villages having the suffix 'St Mary'. Another reason for being dilatory was that, much as I wanted to meet Ray, I could recall nothing but violent quarrels between us. I had tried in Part One of this book to be honest but there often is nothing more offensive than telling the truth. Ray might well consider that the truth, as seen by me, was highly offensive.

On the same day that the *Eastern Daily Press* article was published the *Eastern Evening News* carried a headline:

RAY PARKE PHONES – 'I'M HERE IN NORWICH'

'Oh where oh where has Ray Parke gone?' asked a headline in the Press today. Two hours later Ray Parke — being sought by a group of former R.A.F. colleagues — telephoned Eastern Counties Newspapers to say, 'I'm at the Norwich Union, in the Law Department.'...Said Mr Parke, 'At the time I was with 218 Squadron (1944) I lived at Thorpe St Andrew — they made a mistake with the St Mary, but at least they knew it was a saint'...'I'm going to ring Inspector Browne as he seems to be the contact man,' said Mr Parke, who is now married with two children and lives at Sprowston.

Early on a fine summer morning Audrey and I set off to drive to Norfolk. The roads were clear and we followed the route I had not travelled since the days, before the squadron moved its base to Suffolk, when I would mount the Norton and ride south to see her in London. But such nostalgia as I felt was carefully reined; runaway sentimentality is never far from sadness, and there is no novelty in sorrow.

And yet, against better judgement, we made a short detour to visit the place where Klenner's crew had waited to fly on their first operation and where, during a foggy November, Audrey and I had fallen in love.

I called at the village stores in Methwold to ask exactly where the old aerodrome had been because nothing in the village was familiar. The storekeeper said that I was the third person in three weeks to come looking for the airfield and thought he recognized me. He gave directions and as soon as we began to drive along the right road the years shrivelled and the scenery slotted into place. On the left was the wood which had concealed the crew's Nissen hut, and to the right was a huge black hangar, now surrounded by poppies in bloom. Then, overgrown with weeds and brush, we saw the entrance to the wood which the crew had used daily.

We turned the car and for a few moments looked across the fields in the direction of the airfield. We couldn't see the field itself which lay in a dip but the black roof of another hangar was visible. It was the old maintenance hangar and it was close to its stark outline that Audrey and I had kissed for the first time. But neither of us referred to that other existence when we had lived for the moment, not realizing it was a moment of mutable passion. We said nothing, but we did not have to speak to reaffirm the belief that what perishes is not wasted and that what endures is worth safeguarding.

As we drove back to the village I saw the most familiar landmark of all, a church spire rising delicately above a line of trees. It had been a thing of beauty then, a tranquil background to the Lancasters which had stood like brooding birds of prey in their dispersals, and it was still a thing of beauty.

We arrived at Sprowston, a residential suburb of Norwich, shortly after noon. Ray's house was semi-detached and slightly older than most of the houses in the road; extra rooms had been built at the rear and at the front was a wrought iron gate painted white. He came hurrying out to greet us. We grinned at each other and no one watching us shaking hands would have guessed that once we had enjoyed such a hearty mutual antagonism. There were crease lines round his eyes, but his face was smooth and, apart from an occasional grey hair he had altered very little.

We were introduced to his wife, his sixteen-year-old son and his thirteen-year-old daughter, and we all went into the lounge where Ray poured out glasses of sherry. It was clear that the newspaper items had aroused local curiosity and interest; Ray said that he had received about ten telephone calls on the morning the first article was published. Conversation was disjointed, but enthusiastic. He was keen to know every scrap of news about the other crew members. I asked him whether he had kept fit since the war. 'Oh, yes. I still play hockey for a local team. As goalkeeper.'

'I've looked after him well,' said his wife with a smile.

I asked if he remembered how we used to quarrel bitterly.

He laughed. 'I certainly do.'

'You hated having to "window" when I was with Les.'

'That was a job I loathed. I just used to shove the stuff down the chute, feeling fed up. Then one night I realized I'd gone and mechanically posted my flying rations down it. Posted that precious chocolate away over Germany.'

The children listened raptly, and our wives indulgently, until Audrey suddenly asked, 'Did you have any recurrent nightmares after it was finished?'

Ray looked thoughtful. 'I did have one. I was always just on my way to briefing, and a bit late, but I couldn't seem to get to the briefing room because my flying boots were so heavy.'

I mentioned Dig's deafness and asked if he had suffered any disability. 'Nothing at all,' he said. 'But for a long while I found the days used to drag by and I was bored.' He paused, 'I seem to remember Dig plugged his ears with cotton wool towards the end of the tour.' Then he chuckled. 'I shall never forget the night I shone the aldis lamp right into Dig's face. He nearly blasted me out of the aircraft. Said I'd ruined his night vision and he wouldn't be able to see anything.'

'What were you doing with an aldis lamp?'

'I was setting it up for you. You had to shine it on the ground ahead so that Dig could see his way out of the dispersal and then get to the end of the runway.'

I had forgotten that there were no lights anywhere on the airfield except the thin lines of runway lights which could be switched off at a moment's warning if there were enemy aircraft overhead, and I had forgotten that it had been my job to light our path.

We went in two cars to a nearby hotel for lunch. The dining-room was pleasant with panelled walls and a high ceiling but the service was poor and long before the end of the meal Ray became restive. 'I don't mind taking *my* time over a meal,' he said, 'But I don't see why I should take *their* time.'

We eventually returned to his house and he and I went to sit in a canvas shelter in the garden. He told me that he had volunteered for aircrew because he wanted to catch up with his best friend who was a year older and training to be a flight engineer. He would happily have been an air gunner, which was a shorter course, but was told he was too heavy for this trade and so he chose to be an engineer instead. At the selection interview he was asked if he knew what an engine cotter-pin was, and he described the cotter-pin on a bicycle. There

156

was no similarity between the two types of cotter-pin but he was passed as fit for training as an engineer. In eight months he had to learn what in civil aviation is a four-year course. But he never caught up with his best friend who was killed on ops before Ray joined our crew.

I asked if he had been afraid very often. 'I can't remember ever being really afraid,' he said. 'I was the baby of the crew and it was all a big adventure.' He thought for a few moments. 'The nearest I came to being afraid was when my sleeve got torn by flak. What raid was that?'

'Gelsenkirchen,' I said, and I knew that if it had been my sleeve the name 'Gelsenkirchen' would have been inscribed on my memory until death.

He pondered on the question of fear. He had, he said, forgotten so much. He had a vivid memory of Les warming his hands on a mug of tea at breakfast each day but it was difficult to remember anything about the flying. And there had been a completely blank period in his life which had begun the day we finished flying and lasted for three months. He had absolutely no recollection of anything which happened during those three months.

On the whole he thought the period with the crew was a good time, but he had never really thought about it. The three month curtain of total forgetfulness made everything about operational flying rather remote.

Now that we were talking, he said, he could remember the diversion to St Eval. In particular he remembered the Mustang which had stayed protectively close. Its pilot had amused him by giving a victory sign when the English coastline came into sight and then sheering off.

We fell silent and I looked at the water lilies growing in a little pond he had constructed in the garden. 'I can tell you when I was most ashamed,' he said suddenly.

'Yes, tell me.'

'It was on that trip to Walcheren Island to bomb the German batteries on the coast. It was a Sunday morning. A lovely fine morning. We had just dropped our bombs and were turning for home when I looked out and saw a pall of smoke rising from the middle of a town − Middelburg was its name − and I knew the smoke must have

157

come from a bomb. I thought, "Who could drop a bomb on the town just when people were coming out of church?" and I felt very ashamed.'

He couldn't remember anything about Dresden except the fires and didn't recall that refugees had been mentioned at the briefing.

'Was it all worth it?' I asked.

He gave a short laugh. 'Was it all worth it?' he repeated. 'That's a difficult question. It was an experience I wouldn't have missed. But was it worth it? In a way, I suppose the answer is no. But I'm not sure. I'm not sure.'

'Who can be sure?'

I gathered up my papers and we rose to walk back to the house.

'You told me you'd been with the Norwich Union since your demob,' I said. 'What exactly is your position there?'

'I'm a legal executive in the solicitors' office.'

We rejoined Audrey and his family and his wife set about making a pot of tea.

'Of course,' said Ray suddenly, as though it were a left-over remark from a previous conversation, 'Old Dig was like a father to us.'

I handed him Part One of the book. 'George and Les have read it and approved,' I said. 'Let me know what you think.' And I told him not to hesitate to say if he found any of the passages between himself and me inaccurate.

He gave a half-grin, 'I'm going to look forward to reading this,' he said.

Dear Mike,

It was really good to see you both again after such a long time, and we very much look forward to seeing you and the others later on. I did enjoy recalling those times, and it was only after talking to you that I realized just how much I had completely forgotten.

In fact, since our talk, and reading the book, I have been wondering whether quite unrealized until this time my mind had set up a defence mechanism which shut out all sensibilities and realism. You will remember that I could not recall anything of the immediate post-operational period.

I wouldn't want you to change anything on my account. You've done a great job, and I enjoyed it very much. God, what a rag-bag bunch we were. The relationship between you and me came over very much more strongly than I remembered. Indeed, on further reflection this must have been another aspect of the tensions and anxieties which my mind had rejected...

Best wishes,
Yours,
Ray.

Since meeting Ray again I have wondered why we were so furiously antipathetic. Possibly the only irreconcilable difference between us was that while he was busy showing me he wasn't afraid of hard work, even if I was, I was working busily to show him, and everyone else, that I wasn't afraid.

7. *Paul*

PAUL'S WHEREABOUTS was still a problem. George was trying through police contacts in Liverpool to find out something, and now Ray was in the hunt because he was honorary secretary to a local association connected with the fish trade. He hoped through his contacts to discover what had happened to former traders in the Liverpool fish market.

My gloomy task was to search through the indexes of deaths at Somerset House. On the second-floor balcony lined with records of registered mortality I went through sixty heavy volumes spanning the years since I had last seen Paul. There were two deaths of Songests in Liverpool; one in 1956 of a child less than a year old called Philip, and one in 1966 of a man called Claude B. Songest who had died aged seventy-three. Was it possible that the man had been Paul's father and that Paul himself was the registered 'informant of death'? If so, Paul's 1966 address would appear on the death certificate. I paid a small fee and applied for a copy death certificate to be sent to me. It seemed a long shot but in the past Paul had gambled much more money on the improbable turn of a card.

It seemed so unlikely that the long shot would score that before receiving the death certificate I wrote to the editor of the *Liverpool Echo* to see whether a story similar to *Oh where oh where has Ray Parke gone?* could be run. Then the certificate arrived and it showed that Paul was the 'informant' and gave an address in Dawlish, Devon. I sent a telegram asking him to telephone me as soon as possible and reverse the charges, and I hoped fervently that he had not moved house since 1966.

He rang at one o'clock in the afternoon and didn't reverse the charge. I told him briefly the reason for the telegram and asked if I could come and see him. 'Sure,' he said, 'that'd be lovely.'

'One week-end perhaps?'

'Any time. But I'm moving next month.'

'How about this coming week-end?'

'Fine.'

'Do you work five days a week, Monday to Friday?'

'Why?'

'I was wondering about coming down on Friday.'

'Why not? I've got my own business. I can clear off any time.'

'You don't seem to have altered at all.'

'I don't think I have,' he said.

In George Harrison's regular 'Over the Mersey Wall' feature in the *Liverpool Echo*, run under a four-column headline of 'Calling Paul Songest' the story of the search for the crew appeared. It evoked an immediate response and on the following day George Harrison wrote sending me Paul's address which had been supplied by a reader of his column. I could have saved myself the trouble of obtaining a death certificate. Once again the Press had demonstrated that the phrase 'power of the Press' was no idle boast.

The sea was shimmering blue under a perfect sky, and the cliffs seemed to have been moulded out of terra-cotta by a superhuman sculptor, as the train drifted to a halt at Dawlish. On the platform Paul was waiting with his seven-year-old daughter. His hair was almost as grey as mine and his face, much older now, seemed as undernourished as ever.

On our way to his house I asked what his business was. 'Antiques, junk,' he replied. In a sense the antique trade began with dealers like him, he said. He would offer to clear a house for an agreed sum and then a process of sorting began. Occasionally when an item took his fancy − and his fancy was for eighteenth- and nineteenth-century seascape paintings and old silver − he would keep it for himself;

some of the remainder he would sell to other dealers, and the rest, the rubbish, he would dispose of as refuse. He had a shop at the back of town, run by himself and his seventeen-year-old son, which sold old plates, chests of drawers and other articles which had a market among people who wanted to furnish and let rooms to holiday makers.

We sat in a lounge overlooking the sea while his wife made tea. The room was full of fascinating furniture and the walls were covered with paintings which reflected Paul's taste; in particular he liked a river scene by John Wallace Tucker, a beach scene by Henry Rodmore, and a seascape by Thomas Luny. A Victorian doll's house built into a large glass fronted cabinet and lavishly furnished with tiny inlaid furniture was an obvious collector's item, as was the French music-box with an inlaid top and, inside, a drum and bells in addition to the usual cylinder. Indeed, wherever one looked there was something to please and interest the eye.

He had entered the antique business by chance. After leaving Liverpool some fourteen years ago he and his wife, with a daughter of five and a son of three, had tried to run a small-holding in North Wales. But it rained incessantly and after two miserable years they decided to move south. 'I had no job. Nothing,' said Paul.

He began dealing in junk in Teignmouth and when business began to prosper he moved to Dawlish. Things had improved all the time and it was quite clear that he would never again be in need.

'When you visited me in 1952 you said life was one long holiday,' I remarked.

'It still is. I make it one. If I feel like fishing I go fishing. I've got a small boat. I just hang up a notice on the shop door "Gone fishing".'

After drinking a cup of tea with us Paul's wife had left the room to start preparing dinner. I told him the news of the crew and that I had been drinking with Harry in the lunch-hour yesterday. Harry had suggested that we should by hook or crook try to get Dig to England for a reunion. 'That would be marvellous,' said Paul.

'The air fare would cost a lot.'

'You can count on me in any whip round,' he said.

I mentioned Dig's deafness and asked Paul if he had suffered apart from ulcers.

'The ulcers were enough. I drew a Ministry of Pensions disability pension for twelve years for ulcers caused by flying.'

'How are you now?'

'Much better but they still play me up occasionally.'

I handed him a draft of Part One and asked if he would read it as soon as possible so that I could send it to Dig. He flicked over the pages and scanned the chapter headings. 'The bombing of Dresden,' he said and gave a sour smile.

'You remember it?'

'Of course.'

'Do you remember the briefing?'

'I remember we were told it was more or less chock-a-block with refugees. At the time it had virtually no impact on me. I was most interested because it was to be our longest flight.'

'Have you read *The Destruction of Dresden* by David Irving?'

'Yes.'

'How did you like it?'

'It was a bit too statistical for my liking. A bit boring.'

'Did it worry you what he wrote?'

'Not particularly.'

'Does the raid itself worry you. With hindsight, I mean.'

'I think it was unnecessary. It was slaughter for slaughter's sake. I mean, it was so near the end of the war, bombing Dresden didn't make any difference. It wasn't like Hiroshima. I think *that* bombing really did stop a war and save thousands of lives. Even though lives in Hiroshima were lost. But Dresden wasn't in the same category.'

'You remember it over the target area?'

'Yes. We saw one or two Russian fighters, you know.'

'I don't remember.'

'We thought they were Russian fighters. They were flying along with the stream.'

Paul was in the mood for talking and we were alone. He said he had volunteered for aircrew because his friends had done so, and he preferred flying to 'getting stuck in the mud.' He meant the French and Belgian mud of World War I and I wondered how many of our generation, reared on stories of gangrened bodies and rat-infested trenches, had chosen the air or the sea to avoid what was in reality an already obsolescent type of warfare.

'Did it change you in any way — your nature or temperament?'

He thought hard. 'That's almost impossible to answer. What a question to ask! How do I know whether I would have been any different?'

'Vague questions sometimes bring out more than concise ones which get a "yes" or "no" answer.'

'I can see that. But I can't answer this one. I can only say it was an experience I wouldn't have missed. Those who came through were done more good than harm. We were able to meet people from every walk of life from coal miners to company directors and professional men...Anyway, if you can stick five years in the Forces, you can certainly put up with anything afterwards.'

'Were you afraid?'

'Perpetually.'

I laughed. 'Not perpetually, Paul.'

'Well, I can't say I was walking about knock-kneed. I was apprehensive some of the time and frightened at odd times. I can't remember any specific instances.'

'What was the worst raid for you then?'

His eyes were fixed on a pair of Staffordshire china dogs but it was the gaze of a man looking inward. 'Strangely enough,' he said, 'the worst raid was one I did without the crew. Early in our tour I flew once as a spare bod with another crew. Their mid-upper was unfit for flying that day, I think. As we came up to the target the pilot told us all to put on our parachutes. That scared me stiff. I knew I'd slung mine inside the kite somewhere but I didn't know where. It wasn't till it was all over that I wondered if this particular crew always wore their parachutes over a target. It might have been their routine. And the target was a bit of a warm one.'

I asked him for log-book details of the raid.

'The pilot was Fl. Lieut O'Brien, aircraft J-Jig, daylight, Homberg, four hours fifteen minutes.'*

* Sadly, when I tried to trace Fl. Lieut O'Brien, I learned that he had died some eighteen months before. His widow informed me that he had stomach trouble by the end of his tour and, after post-operational leave, he was admitted to the station hospital for treatment. Mrs O'Brien did not know whether his sudden death from coronary thrombosis was in any way attributable to operational flying.

'No other really bad raids?'

'Well, there was Witten, of course. And I always remember the overshoots at St Eval...When we were coming back, and flying towards St Eval, we flew down the coastline. It looked beautiful and it was *this* coastline. I've always remembered what it looked like, and now I'm living with it.'

'Why did we disband after agreeing to have reunions?'

'Laziness basically. We were too lazy to bother.'

'Final question, Paul. In view of the world situation today was the Allied effort in '39-'45 worth it?'

'Yes. It had to be done. With all the atrocities in Germany it had to be done. But who actually *won* the war I wouldn't like to say.'

For a while we sat reminiscing and then his son returned from the shop. Paul jumped to his feet to introduce us. 'Michael meet Michael,' he said. Then his daughter, Josephine, who was training to be a hairdresser, came home and we all had dinner. After the meal he sat by a window reading a draft of the book while the rest of us watched television.

I slept in the spare room and on the following morning Paul and I went to look round a house he had to clear. It stank of old age and the accumulation of stale odours. There was dust, dereliction and hoarded junk everywhere. But among the rubbish were one or two things of value. Paul pulled open a drawer and took out an old cigarette packet. 'You can't afford to miss anything,' he said opening the packet and drawing out a string of artificial pearls. I found a small box of cheap jewellery, and among the tawdry rings and brooches was a head from a stalk of corn. What was it doing among an old lady's treasures? Had it been given to her many years before by a boy whom she had loved while they walked through a field of corn? I could see that Paul's job was not for the sentimental.

'It's ninety-five per cent for cash,' he said. 'But you could write a book about it.'

'I wouldn't begin to know how to start clearing this mess.'

'Michael and I will have it done in an evening.'

We returned to his house to watch the morning play in the fourth England-Australia Test Match on television. I was due to leave in the afternoon but we had booked a call to Australia for 2.30 p.m. and in between watching cricket we talked about the crew and of Dig in particular. More than once Paul said he was staggered by the insight shown by Dig in his long letter. 'He just wasn't the sort of man to write letters...And to write such a letter...'

I suggested that perhaps the letter was more than just a communication to his former bomb-aimer; in some ways, with its tribute to his father and the hopes expressed for his children, it had the ring of a testament of faith.

'For a man who hates letter-writing it was a bloody good letter, anyway,' said Paul.

The call to Australia came shortly after BBC television had switched from cricket to horse racing at Ascot. Dig's voice at the other end of the line was strong and clear. I told him Paul had been traced and handed the telephone to Paul. Dig's delighted greeting was clearly audible two yards away. We asked, if a passage could be arranged, whether he would be free to come to England. He liked the idea but sounded doubtful. He was tied up on a works project for the next six or eight months and a tight schedule had to be kept. Before closing I said, 'If you're interested in the Test cricket, Graveney and Fletcher are both out.'

There was a slight pause. 'The actual score at this moment,' said Dig, 'is England are 235 for 5.'

As Paul said later, 'Ringing Australia is rather an expensive way of getting an up to the moment score just because television has switched to racing at Ascot.'

On the journey back to London I remembered something Paul had said, quite out of the blue. He had turned from watching the cricket to say, 'Of course you and I were different from the others. We were by far the most irresponsible in the crew.'

It was a truth I had overlooked.

8. *'Mike'*

WHEN THE WAR in Europe finished a number of non-commissioned aircrew were demoted to the rank of A.C.2 and sent to R.A.F. centres to retrain for different trades. This coldly bureaucratic demotion of men who had served their country was a shabby chapter in the history of the R.A.F. The psychological effect of switching from flying in an offensive which was vital for victory to being down-graded so that one could be ordered to do this and do that by a corporal who had never flown in his life was devastating. My own experience was humiliating. I arrived at Cranwell, the first of a host of demoted aircrew, and because I was the first the authorities didn't know what to do with me. I was billeted with a number of recently mustered young airmen and they were as bewildered as I to find a flight sergeant who had completed a tour of operations in their midst. Because the policy of demotion had not been publicized they not unnaturally thought that I had gone L.M.F. during my tour and this was my punishment. They just did not believe that a man could honourably complete a tour of operations and end up as an A.C.2.

It wasn't until other demoted aircrew arrived that my position improved. We were then all billeted together and told that off-duty we could wear the badges of rank held during flying duties, but because there was general resentment at the way we had been treated we did everything possible to make a nuisance of ourselves and, I am glad to say, we succeeded fairly well. The flagpole of the parade ground was burned down and we went absent without leave *en masse* when the war in the Far East finished. At one time I was on five different charges for conduct prejudicial to good order and discipline. All this may seem rather childish nearly a quarter of a century later, but at the time we were consumed with indignation, and the rancour of being treated as I was during those first few days at Cranwell has never quite left me. I could not now ever recommend anyone to volunteer for dangerous duties in the service of Great Britain without warning him that once his usefulness was over he must expect to be treated as scrap material.

I returned to studying law after demobilization and found it difficult to settle to this sort of work. When a government grant ran out in 1949, with only the intermediate exam passed, I took on a full-time job as a solicitor's clerk in an office in Stamford, Lincolnshire, and began a correspondence course with law tutors. By this time Audrey and I were married and we had two children, Ann and David. On my weekly pay of six pounds we lived rather badly. Poverty is an erosive of love and I shall never be convinced that a marriage is enhanced by worries about money, or that sharing cash difficulties binds man and wife more closely together. However, eventually the final exams were passed and my salary was increased to ten pounds per week. At the age of twenty-seven I was finally on my way. Soon after this our third and last child, Brenda, was born.

Because this is a book about seven men in war and the same seven men many years later, there is no point in writing more about myself except to answer those questions which were asked of the others and have not been answered elsewhere.

Before demobilization I had pains in my back and legs diagnosed as fibrositis, and I was medically reclassified as C3 — fit for duties in the U.K. only. These pains continued, on and off, for a number of years but it wasn't until 1958 that ankylosing spondylitis was diagnosed. By this time my spine was totally rigid, the gristle between each vertebra having ossified to bone. I was unable to walk without pain, but how much of the pain was psychosomatic I cannot tell. It is a fact that shortly after my son was taken to hospital with schizophrenia I had to take daily dosages of codeine.

I never tried to claim a pension for this disability but the orthopaedic specialist who treated me said that flying had probably caused the complaint although the precise cause of the disease is unknown, as indeed is its cure. He said that physical tension over a prolonged period seemed to predispose people to ankylosis and said that many prisoners of war in Japanese hands had suffered from it. It is also the somewhat bizarre occupational disease of Indian fakirs.

As to whether the war was worth the fighting, I believed then, and still believe, that had Nazi Germany won the war the world would now be in an even worse mess. The British and Americans may be accused by Negroes and other coloured peoples of being 'racialist' but there are no extermination camps in the United Kingdom or the United States and this surely would have been their fate in a world dominated by Nazi ideology. If the only merit in the Allies winning the war was that Nazi gas chambers were abolished, it is sufficient merit. I am sorry that my bombs killed many, and made many homeless, but I am not ashamed. If a malignant growth must be cut out, without benefit of anaesthetic, then surrounding tissues are bound to be hurt. I was simply a small part of the scalpel.

As for the bombing of Dresden, I must make it clear that I am not a heroic figure who deliberately disobeyed orders. There was no Master Bomber on the air and so I tried to dispose of my bombs so that they fell harmlessly clear, but had a Master Bomber instructed crews to stoke up fires (the usual practice when no pinpoint targets were available) I am fairly sure that I should have directed Dig to fly over the heart of the city instead of its southern extremity. When David Irving was collecting material for his book *The Destruction of Dresden* I was one of the many participating aircrew whom he interviewed. I asked him about the Master Bomber and some time later he wrote in a letter — 'I have found out more about the Master Bombers of the two Dresden attacks. One is now chief editor of *Flight*, the other, the Master Bomber during your attack, a Canadian, was bomb-aimer in the only Pathfinder Lancaster of the 61 dispatch which did not return.' It was now clear why there had been no Master Bomber on the air. He had been killed.[19]

I thought *The Destruction of Dresden* a better book than Paul found it. So far as I can tell it was completely accurate except for a mistake as to the probable number of people killed, a mistake caused through no lack of diligence on the author's part, but due to the unwillingness of the East German authorities to release the correct figures. It now seems that a reliable estimate of the number killed may be 25,000, and not as was conjectured, 100,000. But this statistic, necessary for historical accuracy, is meaningless to human imagination. One cannot work out a multiplication table for tragedy. I thought that in the fourth part of his book the author dwelt a little too lingeringly on the aftermath of the raid; it came perilously near horror for the sake of horror rather than for the sake of humanity.

It is a curious fact that moral outrage in a country varies inversely with the prevailing climate of war and peace in that country; that is to say, when a country is committed to war its moral outrage is directed at what another country, its enemy, has done or is doing, but when it is at peace it directs its sense of moral outrage inwardly and like some penitent *roué* beats its chest at the memories of past sins. When Sir Arthur Harris published his book *Bomber Offensive* in which it was made clear that the R.A.F. had bombed whole cities by saturation rather than by pinpointing specifically military targets there followed a wave of protest by church leaders and others concerned with moral leadership, but it is curious fact that these people were notably silent when the outrage of saturation bombing was being committed – and it will not hold water to say that they did not know. Thousands of aircrew and ground crew knew, so why didn't they? Nor will it hold water to say they were muzzled. Such a volume of opinion could not have been stemmed by King Canute or Winston Churchill. The plain fact is that when one's survival is threatened, in some shape or form, one is grateful to those who offer protection, but once the danger is past one is ashamed that one's intellectual theories were so easily overruled by a primitive instinct or emotion, and the erstwhile helpers are an immediate target for the hostility caused by this sense of shame. Everyone knows (and certainly the Americans must know after helping Britain in two world wars) that the best way of making a peacetime enemy is to give practical help in time of war. No one loves his creditor.

It has not been easy to write this brief chapter on the crew's bomb-aimer, but mercifully we never see ourselves as others see us. It is a disastrous exercise in the vanity of self-mortification to be too objective about oneself. But if a picture has emerged of a man whose inferiority complex has driven him to prove things that have required no proof, who has always been fascinated by the diversity and vagaries of human nature, and who enjoys writing about people, I would ask for no better likeness.

9. A Summing-up

ALL ABBREVIATIONS DISTORT. The précis, however well constructed must slightly distort the original; the slogan always distorts the précis. A religious slogan such as 'God is Love' may comfort the emotions of millions but it does not satisfy the intellect. One might as well say, as Samuel Butler did in one of his *Notebooks*, 'Love is God'. Both slogans have an equally fine ring and if repeated often enough seem to epitomize profound universal truths, and yet who can describe God, and who can define love, so that God and love are neatly balanced on the see-saw of a philosophical equation?

All slogans are attractive if they seem to mirror a truth which for some reason − lack of affection, lack of security − we need to believe, and the effect of oft-repeated slogans on the human mind is enormous whether coined as a formula for self-help (e.g. Émile Coué's 'Every day, in every way, I am getting better and better,') or as a formula for sales promotion (e.g. 'Guinness is good for you'). Unfortunately we are so impressed by the slogan we scarcely ever take the trouble to search for the motives of those who are promoting the slogan.

Political agitators know well how to reduce a complex issue to a simple emotive slogan and then use the slogan as a weapon for their own ends. 'Stop American fascism in Vietnam' is a somewhat long-winded, but nevertheless successful, slogan which does not begin to convey the problem which in five words it is both attempting to present and to solve.

I have laboured this point because in summarizing the foregoing chapters I found facile slogans coming to mind and was almost beguiled by their apparent aptness into thinking that the crew could be presented as seven archetypes. They seemed to fall so neatly into categories. Dig, for example, was the father-leader. Paul was the

171

have-a-go gambler. Harry was the civilized coloured man caught in cross-currents of race and class. Les was the reliably still waters which run deep. George was the loyal team man. Ray was the youngest crew member on his first big adventure. And I was the odd man out who observed all the others. And these easy labels are not true but neither are they false. They are false true, and if this oxymoron sounds like another slogan at least the motive behind it is not political, religious or auto-suggestive. It is to make clear that the honesty I have tried to bring to this book falls far short of ideal honesty, and the truth I have tried to present falls far short of ideal truth. If I have overstressed this obvious fact it is because the six men described in this book did not ask to be written about, or analysed, and I would not wish them to carry my slick labels round their necks or to be hung by the noose of conclusions in this chapter.

From interviews and correspondence it is clear that the stress of flying forty operations did produce some subsequent ill health. Nothing much was known in the 1940s of stress-induced diseases, and almost too much is known in the 1960s so that nearly every illness can be loosely related to stress, but out of seven men four have suffered from stomach troubles, one has become deaf, and one has a rigid spine probably caused by tension. These figures prove nothing but they may be an indication that damage to the body can continue long after the conditions of stress have finished. For some of us it took two or three years to settle down mentally, but it has taken our bodies much longer. That physical illness can come as a delayed reaction to mental stress, sometimes very many years after the cause of the stress has been removed, is, I understand, something which medical science is at present investigating.

During the war medical research for the benefit of aircrews was almost exclusively directed at alleviating one particular type of stress – fatigue, which included muscular fatigue, mental fatigue and skill fatigue. The long-term effects of physiological and psychological tension among aircrews was not considered. Fatigue was the immediate and obvious bogey. Provided crews were taught how to recognize symptoms of fatigue, and combat them, this was all that mattered. A variety of drugs were tested to see how far these could prevent, or stave off, the fatigue which was inevitable if a crew was obliged to fly on consecutive days or nights. Caffeine was useful in helping to overcome sleepiness, but the preferred drug was benzedrine in small doses of 5 to 10 milligrams. In theory, benzedrine tablets were to be issued infrequently and only under careful medical direction; in practice, one could simply ask for one or two 'wakey-wakey' pills after every briefing. I built up a small store of benzedrine at one time as an insurance against falling asleep when I was off duty and enjoying myself.

Enormous advances have been made since 'wakey-wakey' pills were the answer to every flyer's problem. There now exists a branch of medicine known as Aviation Medicine in which, since 1967 in Britain, postgraduate diplomas can be taken. Research in this subject deals with such matters as studies on lung mechanics during acceleration and the breathing of oxygen, the interaction between rotation and linear acceleration, the relation between physiological and psychological responses in an aircraft, and the metabolic effect of work load and fatigue. The importance of such research cannot be over-estimated when it is borne in mind that about one-half of all aircraft accidents are attributable to human error and that such error may result from any number of marginal stresses. But for me, and many others, this research is a quarter of a century too late.

Nearly all the crew looked back on the days of operational flying, without qualification, as good times; and such qualification as there was took the form of 'It was an experience I wouldn't have missed for anything.' And the majority opinion, not surprisingly, was that the war effort had been worth while, although Paul did remark 'who actually *won* the war I wouldn't like to say' and Ray said, 'I'm not sure, I'm not sure' and Dig in answer to a further letter I wrote to him has replied, 'The present strife in the world is most upsetting and my secret fear is that my boys will be required to fight in some future area of unrest when of age.'

As for targets, the almost unanimous opinion was that the daylight raid on Witten had remained most vividly in the memory. I wrote to Air Historical Branch (R.A.F.) of the Ministry of Defence and asked whether there were any official records of the raid and what the Lancaster losses were. When the reply came four months later it was terse and to the point. 'Eight bombers were lost on the Witten raid of 12th December 1944. There are no accounts of the raid available for study.'

Paul, who watched the havoc wreaked on the bomber stream by German fighters, thought that many more than eight Lancasters went down over the target, but he couldn't give an alternative estimate. Anyway, the matter once so topical is now of academic interest only.

An unexpected offshoot of the search was the discovery that, Harry excepted, everyone had stayed close to home. Dig was then and is now in Adelaide; Les was then and is now in Sheffield; Ray was then and is now in the vicinity of Norwich; George was then and is now in the West Riding of Yorkshire; I was then and am now in Hertfordshire; and Paul, although he now lives in Dawlish, was for eight years after the war in his home town of Liverpool.

No significant conclusion can be drawn, from such a small sample, about the strongly rooted dwelling habits of ordinary men, and how, even though their lives are disrupted by war, they tend to return to their home territory and stay there. The return may be for social or economic reasons and might also be a part of the territorial imperative (to borrow the graphic phrase coined by the ethologist, Robert Ardrey) but it remains a strange coincidence, if nothing more, that the six white members of the crew returned to their homes and the seventh, a coloured man from Jamaica, made a new home in England. From this tiny sample one might tentatively conclude that the average white man is content with his home, or territory, and the average coloured man is not.

If this conclusion is approximately correct the fears of many that a future conflict will not be between nation and nation, but between

174

race and race, would seem to be justified. Wars can be disguised as religious crusades or as a collision of political ideologies but fundamentally every war is concerned with obtaining control over a new territory, or defending one's own territory from the control of a stranger.

Although Dig had some subsequent reservations, the only two men opposed to the Dresden raid were Paul and me, and we alone in the crew can remember being informed at briefing that Dresden was full of refugees. The others do not recall this part of the briefing and for them the raid was, and remains, a job that had to be done. And yet this is strange because, as Paul perceptively remarked, he and I were 'by far the most irresponsible in the crew'.

During the search it was evident that the idea of tracing missing people appeals to almost everyone, and perhaps this is why such themes are so popular in detective and suspense stories. Also, it became clear that an immense comradeship, like an unseen network of goodwill, connects all those who once served in Bomber Command. The item in the *Eastern Daily Press* about the search for Ray unexpectedly sparked off this goodwill.

Shortly after the article appeared I received a letter from Mr Stanley Hurd of Bradford. He had read about the search and told me he had been a member of ground crew on 218 Squadron and had worked mainly on C-Charlie and D-Dog. From further correspondence, I learned that he had known Jock Henderson, of A-Able, well. Eventually, through his help, and with the help of another former ground crew sergeant, Freddie Wilson, Jock was traced.

I wrote to him at an address in Scotland. In reply he told me he had begun his career with 218 Squadron in 1940 and had remained with the squadron throughout the war, seeing it progress from Fairey

Battles to Blenheims, then to Wellingtons, then to Stirlings, and finally to Lancasters. The war finished and the squadron was disbanded. Jock continued his R.A.F. service and in 1959 was sent to California to train on Thor missiles. In due course he was posted back to England and to his amazement found that 218 Squadron had been resurrected and he was once more to serve with it. Thus he has the unique record of having been on this squadron from Fairey Battles to Thor missiles.

In passing he mentioned that the new location of 218 Squadron had been at North Luffenham in Rutland, and this was a coincidence of a sort because it was in the village next to North Luffenham aerodrome that Audrey and I had lived for a while and where we had been visited by Paul in 1952. But life is full of 'It's a small world' stories which can if pursued lead to all sorts of unanswerable conjectures about Fate, or God, or coincidence, or luck. I was very glad to have heard from Jock again; after all, Klenner's crew owed their survival in no small measure to the work and over-work of him and his small band of ground crew.

A few days later he rang to say he was in London. He had read Part One of the book and wanted to meet me. The following evening he came to our house for dinner.

His face had been toughened by experience and age, and I might not have recognized him had he not smiled, but I remembered his smile and the rest of his face matched itself, feature by feature, against my imperfect memory until full recognition twisted a key and I was again with A-Able's ground sergeant. 'By God, Mike, you've gone grey,' he said.

We talked flying before, during and after dinner and I was surprised at his memory; the book had triggered off a wealth of reminiscence. He handed me some notes he had made on the train journey down from Scotland. One of these read:

> The day you diverted to St Eval was a torment to me. I remember watching the take-off towards Bury and a puff of steam from the port outer made me exclaim to the ground crew 'It looks like we're developing an internal coolant leak.' As you didn't return early with a hot motor I thought it must have been my imagination but when you never returned, and

communications were such that we waited hours for confirmation of the diversion, I was really worried.

The use of the word 'we' reveals better than anything the degree of his identification with Klenner's crew.

Perhaps there has been too much emphasis on fear in this book, and it is difficult to differentiate between fear and acute nervousness, but the candour of the replies to the question 'Were you afraid?' gives a fair indication that the crew was often afraid and yet, at the time, the matter was never discussed. Nobody overhearing arguments on the intercom would have thought that fear was an eighth passenger on board.

I wouldn't go so far as Dig and say that 'a man would have to be stupid or a liar that under those circumstances claimed to be without fear.' Ray did not remember being particularly afraid and he is neither stupid nor a liar. But, perhaps significantly, he did have a recurrent anxiety nightmare. Happily, in Britain nowadays, a man can openly state he is afraid of something and there are few who will scoff at him. During the 1939-45 war this was not so.

It was not until three or four years after the end of the war that pieces about the psychological strain of flying a tour of operations began to appear in newspapers and learned periodicals. Chapman Pincher began a newspaper article − 'The belief that R.A.F. combat crews were fearless daredevils thirsting for action is shattered by a medical report published last night. An Air Force psychologist who watched aircrews on and off duty reveals that even the most reliable pilots were always afraid.' The report Mr Pincher referred to was a *Journal of Medical Science* report and the psychologist was Dr David Stafford-Clark who had discovered that on a tour of thirty operations a man's morale, starting at high, rose slightly at first because of the excitement, but then declined steadily going very close to 'crack-up' level at about the twelfth operation. When the thirteenth operation had been passed morale rose very slightly until about the twenty-second sortie when it dipped, and continued to dip towards 'crack-up' level. Dr Stafford-Clark pointed out in his report that superstition played a valuable part in maintaining a flyer's morale. The man who flew with his girl-friend's silk stocking really believed it would protect him against flak and enemy fighters. Men who had joined simply for the glamour of being R.A.F. aircrew usually cracked up fairly quickly; the others survived to be frightened time and time again.

If there is any conclusion to be drawn it is that men who must become warriors because of the national need in most cases successfully act the part of fearless warriors. The versatility of humanity never fails to amaze me; from birth to death we act some sort of part or another, and it is only those who can't follow the script or don't understand the stage directions who may suffer, and they will usually either end as acclaimed innovators or under treatment in a mental hospital. So long as a man can act a convincing part he is regarded as a normal man, and it is imperative that while the act is on stage we all pretend that it is real, and not make-believe. Klenner's crew acted their part well; they can now sit back in the wings and compare notes about what they really felt.

I think it was generally accepted among Bomber Command aircrew that the odds in favour of survival were not very high, and this was confirmed after the war when Sir Arthur Harris wrote in the *Evening Standard* on the 11th December 1946 – 'Bomber Command's far-reaching successes were not gained without grievous casualties. During the whole period of war approximately 125,000 members of aircrew entered Bomber Command units. During the period of my Command alone it is estimated that nearly 44,000 men were killed, about half that number injured, and more than 11,000 men were held prisoner.' Sir Arthur Harris's command began in February 1942.

But from conversations with the crew, and other flyers, again and again the theme 'You don't think it can happen to you' occurred. George summed up the feelings of thousands of aircrew when he said, 'It was a sort of elated fright…You stood in the astrodome and you felt all excitement. You thought the man next door was going down but not you.'

A different way of facing the odds was explained in a book published in 1957.* In it the authors wrote:

However slight the strain and no matter how long it took to build up, it was there as a very natural revolt of the human system against repeated exposure to risk, whether present and real or merely potential and imagined. It was there inside each one of us, a secret enemy within. It was as if each of us started with a certain capital, a sum of something − was it fortitude? − which we spent, sometimes over a short period, sometimes over a much longer stretch of time. But when it was gone life became a torment with the spirit flogging on a bankrupt body. That was what we called the twitch...Most of us had come to recognize this state of affairs without saying a great deal about it. We just went about our lives happily enough, maintaining a guarded neutrality with the secret enemy, slapping him down with a joke about the twitch whenever his voice was raised too insistently.

Yet another attitude, but probably less common, was the case where a man faced the prospect of death, thought about it, familiarized himself with it, and accepted it to such a degree that he regarded himself as already dead. The self-induced acceptance that one is already dead while physically still alive is something very close to a philosophy. In his *Confessions* Rousseau wrote, 'I can well say that I did not begin to live until I looked on myself as a dead man.'**

Arthur Koestler has written much the same about applied Zen in which the man who has completed his training 'will continue to live zestfully and apparently unchanged, but he will "*live as one already dead*" − that is, detached and indifferent to success or failure.'***

I never completely achieved 'It won't happen to me' or 'It can and has happened to me' but wavered between the two with ever-lengthening periods of 'It could very easily happen to me' intervening. But when off duty I lived as one already dead. It was a wonderfully liberating feeling.

A question which began to be asked after the war was, 'How could decent men drop bombs in saturation attacks knowing that innocent women and children would be killed?' One reason might be called

Night Fighter by C. F. Rawnsley and Robert Wright (Collins).
** *Confessions* (Penguin edn) at page 218.
*** *The Lotus and the Robot* (Hutchinson) at page 243.

tit-for-tat, or the 'revenge motive' coupled with the feeling that 'It's us or them.' As Les said so succinctly, 'War is war. They hit you and you hit them back.' For our generation Coventry was a potent symbol. This city had been bombed by the Luftwaffe, and civilians killed, on a scale hitherto unknown. And not only was Coventry bombed, but other cities also, where it was obvious that the principal casualties would be 'innocent women and children.' The term 'Coventrating' was invented by the Nazis as a standard of civilian destruction, and population bombing was continued throughout the war by the Germans and reached its apogee in the use of V2s and flying bombs which struck at random. I would not dream of attempting to equate the saturation bombing of Hamburg with the population bombing of Coventry; I am sure professional historians can draw many fine distinctions between the German bombing of British cities and the British bombing of German cities, all that I am suggesting is that when flying on operations, and with flak being pumped into the sky all around, and with the subconscious knowledge of British civilians killed by German bombs, one did not greatly care about the victims of a saturation attack. This may sound callous to anyone who was not physically and emotionally involved at the time, and I would be the first to agree that two wrongs do not make a right, but I am not sure that ethics and moralities are the proper context for the arguments about the horrors of total war.

Rather than say, 'Was it right or wrong?' which is a question that has arisen with the very recent civilization of Man, I would wonder whether, thickly covered with arguments about military necessity, political expediency and religious morality, it is not merely a question of 'Was this chain of destruction caused by a will to survive at all costs?' One way to survive if one is attacked with utter ruthlessness is to fight back with utter ruthlessness; this has nothing to do with civilized notions of right and wrong, it is simply Man's nature and has been part of his instinctual equipment from the time that he began to get on equal terms with other mammals millions of years ago.

Another explanation of how it is perfectly easy to kill innocent women and children is suggested by Konrad Lorenz. In his book *On Aggression* he comments on the fact that Man alone of the entire animal kingdom has invented artificial weapons, and it is these which have upset the innate equilibrium of killing potential and social inhibition which in other species prevents the self-destruction of that species. He writes, 'The distance at which all shooting weapons take effect screens the killer against the stimulus situation which would otherwise activate his killing inhibitions. The deep, emotional layers of our personality simply do not register the fact that the crooking of the fore-finger to release a shot tears the entrails of another man. No sane man would ever go rabbit-hunting for pleasure if the necessity of killing his prey with his natural weapons brought home to him the full emotional realization of what he is actually doing.

'The same principle applies to an even greater degree to the use of modern remote-control weapons. The man who presses the releasing button is so completely screened against seeing, hearing or otherwise emotionally realizing the consequences of his action, that he can commit it with impunity – even if he is burdened with the power of imagination. Only thus can be explained that perfectly good-natured men, who would not even smack a naughty child, proved to be perfectly able to release rockets or lay carpets of incendiary bombs on sleeping cities, thereby committing hundreds and thousands of children to a horrible death in flames. The fact that it is good, normal men who did this is as eerie as any fiendish atrocity of war!'*

And yet…In spite of revenge motives, the prevailing spirit of the times, the instinct to survive at all costs, and the explanation of Konrad Lorenz, did not I make use of a radio silence over Dresden to try and drop my bombs clear of the burning city, and did not Ray say of Middelburg, 'I knew the smoke must have come from a bomb. I thought "Who could drop a bomb on the town just when people were coming out of church?" and I felt very ashamed.'

We were prepared to devastate cities like Essen and Cologne where it was known that among the civilians there were military and quasi-military objectives, but our spirits revolted at the thought of destroying life where there was no immediate military target, and perhaps this revulsion and shame is one measure of Man's progress from the dark beginnings to the present day.

---

* *On Aggression* (Methuen) at page 208.

Epilogue

George 'Dig' Klenner was the only man absent from the first crew reunion which took place in 1969, but a call was put through to Australia and we each spoke to Dig. When the book was reissued in 1978 a mini-reunion at a Norfolk hotel was organized by Les Walker. Only four of the crew were present. When Les, who had been ill for some time, died early in 1982, it seemed certain that there would be no more reunions and if I had been told that a third would be initiated as a result of a chance meeting between a German woman and someone at the Imperial War Museum, neither of whom I knew, it would have been difficult to believe.

The woman was undertaking preliminary research for a television documentary series about the bomber offensive and a member of staff at the Imperial War Museum had suggested to her that she read *The Eighth Passenger*. Weeks later I was telephoned by Erich Bottlinger, a producer with Südwestfunk, who asked me to meet him. After a quick word with Audrey, I invited him and the chief cameraman to lunch at our home.

After the meal he and I adjourned to my study. He told me that he had been commissioned to produce five one-hour documentaries, the last of which was to be about Dresden. He said that Sir Arthur Harris and Group Captain Leonard Cheshire VC had agreed to cooperate in the series and asked if I would take part. The documentaries would provide "an objective picture on history", would contain no "chauvinistic German message", but I would be expected to answer the sort of questions German viewers would ask: "How did you feel knowing that the bombs you dropped on cities would kill civilians?" and "Why did you have to go on destroying our cities when it was obvious to everyone that we had lost the war?"

I told him that during a raid my thoughts were concentrated on

183

survival and when the raid was over it would have been foolish to dwell on its possible consequences – the mental stress of operational flying was already severe enough. This might seem self-centred and insensitive to the suffering of others, but unless one had lived through this period of history it was difficult, if not impossible, to convey the spirit of the times, which demanded complete victory over Nazi Germany at almost any cost. Moreover, there was something impersonal about dropping a load of bombs from four miles up in the sky, particularly when nothing except banks of clouds could be seen below.

I went on to say that if I was expected to express remorse I would not do so. Naturally I regretted that many German civilians had died, but equally I regretted that many British civilians had died from Luftwaffe attacks and the indiscriminate bombing by V2 missiles. Furthermore, in no way would I criticize the men who had flown with Bomber Command on the Dresden raid.

After Erich Bottlinger left I said to Audrey, "I don't think I shall hear any more from him." But I did. He asked if I could arrange a crew reunion and line up sites for filming. Expenses would be paid. I agreed and so, in September, 1983, the crew (with the exception of Les) came together again for the first time since 1945. George Klenner, now retired from General Motors Holdens, flew over from Australia with his wife. Harry, Paul and George had also retired from their respective occupations. Only the youngest, Ray, was still in regular employment.

And so it was that in September, 1983, Audrey and I were filmed strolling along the perimeter of the old airfield at Chedburgh, the place from where we and other crews had taken off for Dresden. The runways had been dug up and the field was now arable land. Following the exterior shots a long interview took place in the old briefing room. This prefabricated building was the only one to have been preserved intact in a complex devoted to the manufacture of chemical fertiliser by a company called Chafter who had kindly given permission for the filming to take place.

Before returning to Germany Erich persuaded Audrey and me to visit Dresden with him. We agreed, but we never got there. One morning in November when I got up to make cups of tea I discovered that quite unexpectedly Audrey had died at some time during the night. I told Erich that I could not face visiting Dresden without her. After all, for me *The Eighth Passenger* was more than the story of an operational aircrew. It also contained a love story. Erich was very sympathetic, but suggested that perhaps I would be willing to visit Dresden accompanied by Wing Commander Maurice Smith, the master-bomber on the first phase of the attack, who like me had recently become a widower. I met Maurice Smith in London. We spoke little about the Dresden raid, but spent most of the time comparing notes on how we were coping with the single state after many years of marriage. Neither of us was keen to revisit the city which still bore the ravages of a brutal bombing assault, and so we mutually agreed not to go.

Erich accepted this decision without demur, but he pressed me strongly to go to Baden-Baden to stay with him and his wife as their guest. I delayed acceptance because I knew he would want to show me the film taken at Chedburgh. But a year after the filming I finally went, and in a television studio watched scenes on the cutting room screen, and saw and heard Audrey again. It was a bit of an ordeal.

I saw other parts of the series. Erich had kept his word. There was no chauvinistic German message. In fact, it was almost the reverse. He and script writer, Jochen von Lang, had devoted the greater part of the first hour's episode to proving that the bombing of civilians had started with Nazi Germany's attacks on Rotterdam, Warsaw and Coventry. The fifth and last episode contained what was to be Sir Arthur Harris's last appearance on television.

He had refused to be interviewed by anyone but Leonard Cheshire. When the two men met, so Erich informed me, it was obvious that Sir Arthur, then a frail old man in his nineties who had difficulty in walking, had enormous respect for the men who had flown on more than a hundred bombing operations. With cameras rolling they had discussed Bomber Command tactics, but much of what was said was of little use in the documentary as Cheshire, in warming up his former leader, had apparently spoken of matters which were not relevant. However, the following emerged with Sir Arthur, thanks to skilful dubbing, speaking as though fluent in German.

"When one says the bombing war had always been directed at the civilian population. Which war is not?

What was the result in past wars? When you killed enough soldiers you created enough misery amongst their families in the opposing nation until it decided to give in.

All major wars are against nations as a whole and are not boxing matches against selected individuals."

On the video tape Sir Arthur appeared tired; he rubbed his forehead with one hand as though trying to summon a fatigued mind to react with its former forcefulness; but weary though he may have been with age and the never-ending attacks on him, the old warrior's words were uttered with stubborn conviction. Others, their freedom made safe by the sacrifices of a former generation, might occupy the moral high ground and indulge in fashionable criticism, but his foundations remained as firm as the abandoned concrete runways in the eastern counties of England down which bomb-laden aircraft had once roared on their way to take-off for Germany.

Within a few months of the interview Sir Arthur died. Some historians have treated him harshly, and frequently unjustly, but among many of the survivors of the crews he commanded he is remembered with some affection. The five-part *Der Krieg der Bomber* was networked throughout West Germany to coincide with the fortieth anniversary of the bombing of Dresden. Its honesty in blaming Germany for starting the cycle of retaliation angered many viewers who regarded the series as tantamount to treachery. There was a storm of protest which Erich and his colleagues weathered.

Due to technological advances there will never be another major war in which crews consisting of seven men will fly over enemy territory in old, four-engined bombers, but reunions of a dwindling number of Bomber Command survivors continue to be held. One such reunion took place at Chedburgh in October, 1992, when the men who had perished on operations from its airfield were honoured by the unveiling of a memorial. Paul, Ray, Harry and I turned up for the occasion and had our own private reunion. George, who had been invited, did not come; and it was not possible for Dig to fly from Australia.

Finally, there is a correction to the text of this book which must be made. Audrey read the original in draft and approved, or perhaps it would be more accurate to say she did not disapprove. However, on one occasion she said she wished I hadn't written that poverty was an erosive of love. It was, she said, an erosive of passion or "romantic love" but not of love. I agreed and promised that if ever *The Eighth Passenger* were republished I would make this distinction clear. Poverty does not erode love, whatever else it might erode. And, I might add, neither does death erode love.

Notes

(1) On 13 October, 1944, Air Chief Marshal Sir Arthur Harris, Commander-in-Chief of Bomber Command, received a directive for an operation code-named "Operation *Hurricane*". The directive spoke of "demonstrating to the enemy in Germany the overwhelming superiority of the Allied Air Forces...against objectives in the densely populated Ruhr". Early on the morning of 14 October the first phase of Operation *Hurricane* was launched. A force of 1013 bomber aircraft (somewhat less than the 1200 mentioned at our briefing) was dispatched by the RAF on the Duisberg raid. For their part in Operation *Hurricane* the American Eighth Air Force sent heavy bombers to targets in the Cologne area. Fourteen British and six American aircraft were lost.

(2) Reporting on the effects of the Duisberg raids in *The Bomber Command War Diaries* by Martin Middlebrook and Chris Everitt (Viking, 1985) the authors write, "Nearly 9,000 tons of bombs had thus fallen on Duisberg in less than 48 hours." Precise details of the effects of the raids proved difficult to obtain but one local report referred to very serious property damage and the burial of a large number of people.

(3) In a letter to me, Mr Alan Brookes, a former navigator with 195 Squadron, states that the three Lancasters, which belonged to his squadron, were not destroyed by a bomb falling from above but by flak. Apparently four Lancasters were flying in such tight formation that when one was hit by flak it exploded with such force that two adjacent aircraft also blew up. The crew of the fourth Lancaster were so shattered by what they had witnessed that after their return to base they refused to fly again on operations. Mr Brookes writes, "I well remember the officers in the crew were grounded but retained their commissions

whilst the NCOs were catagorized "LMF" and reduced to the ranks.

As to "scarecrows", Max Hastings in *Bomber Command* (Michael Joseph, 1979) dismisses the notion that these were shells designed to frighten aircrews. He writes, "There were no such projectiles as "scarecrows". What the crews saw were indeed exploding British aircraft. But to this day many aircrew will not accept this." But if RAF aircrews deceived themselves about the existence of "scarecrows" so also did some American fighter pilots. The German historian, Dr Helmut Schnatz, has sent me some copies of microfilmed US fighter Group mission summaries taken from documents belonging to the US Army Air Force. In one of these the following occurs: "In Ruhr several bursts of peculiar flak. Started with explosion and flame then round balls of fire mushroomed from explosion, burning with heavy black, oil-like smoke as they fell. Original burst at about 25,000 ft."

Of the first raid on Solingen by 176 Lancasters of 3 Group the authors of *The Bomber Command War Diaries* (op.cit.) state that the attack was not successful and the bombing was "badly scattered". However, German reports show that the second raid was "an outstanding success". The authors of the *Diaries* go on to remark that the second raid on Solingen, together with raids on Bochum and the Dortmund-Ems canal, all undertaken within twenty-four hours, "were good examples of the striking power now possessed by Bomber Command". Nevertheless, the German defences could still be effective. 346 (Free French) Squadron lost five out of its sixteen Halifaxes on the Bochum raid.

(4) Our departure on leave was delayed a few hours. The crew, together with other crews, except three who were being briefed to bomb Koblenz, were ordered to report to the maintenance hangar to belt thousands of rounds of .303 ammunition and pack canisters of incendiary bombs. Even the Vicar and administrative officers took part in this exercise which had been brought about by the result of excessive work demands on the regular armourers. These were a handful of men responsible for

bombing up approximately twenty-five Lancasters and supplying ammunition for three times that number of gun turrets. If, during days and nights of ceaseless activity, bomb-loads had not been altered and re-altered so frequently they might not have fallen asleep so often, sometimes on rain-drenched bomb-trailers. As it was, the medical officer had ordered half of them to hospital as cases of acute exhaustion. The raid on Koblenz, which we missed, proved to be one of the most devastatingly effective of the entire war. A fire raid by only 128 Lancasters of 3 Group, using GH, reduced more than half the town virtually to ashes. It was a foretaste of what was to happen three months later in Dresden.

(5) It was on this raid that one Squadron crew, on their first operation, turned back before reaching the French coast because the navigator became frightened and refused to provide further courses to fly. Consequently this crew's sortie had to be aborted. The navigator was a commissioned officer. He was taken off flying duties and eventually posted quietly away. Had he been a non-commissioned officer he would have been stripped of rank and his records endorsed LMF (Lack of Moral Fibre). In May, 1991, I received a letter from Kevin Roberts, an Australian, who was this crew's wireless operator. Mr Roberts informed me that his crew had been allocated another navigator with whom they flew until the end of the war in Europe. In his letter Mr Roberts named all the crew members except for the frightened navigator because, he explained, by his refusal to proceed to the target the navigator "may have saved my life". This compassionate view was, I think, common among most aircrew who thought, "There, but for the grace of God, go I".

(6) LMF is referred to in a number of letters I have received. One of the most touching was from a man, a former air gunner, who still felt his disgrace so keenly that he gave no address and signed himself, "Sincerely, but anonymously, Bob N." He wrote that after his tenth operation he had a strong premonition that he would be killed on the eleventh. He went LMF. His

crew took off on the next sortie with a spare gunner in his place. They did not return. He was stripped of rank and posted to a place where he met others in the same situation. "At Eastchurch," he wrote, "there were genuine nerve cases, and chaps who had escaped from the Continent after being shot down being stripped down to AC2 and dumped. One Warrant Officer pilot shot himself while I was there and the atmosphere was ghastly."

NCOs who were considered unfit for further flying duties because they had gone LMF, or had proved intractably undisciplined, were usually sent to the receiving centre at Eastchurch, a bleak location on the Isle of Sheppey in the Thames estuary. This remote and desolate place had an airfield and living quarters and, pre-1914, had been a base for Royal Naval Air Service flying school, and had been used for experimentation bombs. Later, during the early days of aviation, it was from this airfield that the pioneering flights of Lord Brabazon and C.S. Rolls were made. During the Battle of Britain RAF Eastchurch became a base for a fighter squadron. These days of glory were not to last. Even today the authorities do not welcome enquiries about the men who were detained at Eastchurch until they could be posted to a destination where they would be dumped, rather like nuclear waste, without fear of contamination to others, and information about conditions at Eastchurch are mostly based on anecdotal evidence. In *Bomber Command* (Michael Joseph, 1979) Max Hastings comments, "The Judge-Advocate General of the Forces is implacably unhelpful on enquiries relating to the problems of disciplinary courts martial and LMF." LMF cases were more often than not treated quite ruthlessly. In his book Max Hastings quotes an unamed commander of an RAF bombing station who told him, "I made certain that every case before me was punished by court martial, and where applicable an exemplary prison sentence."

In 1981 I received a letter from a former flight mechanic. He wrote of Eastchurch, "I remember during the war it was the clearing house for LMF cases and often injured (wounded) cases were lumped together and I visited my brother who was taken off aircrew with the first signs of cataract. All these hundreds of aircrew milling about and the farmers used to pay a shilling an hour to work in the fields..."

Another fragment of information came to me from a correspondent who was a Mosquito navigator and, after the war, a private investigator. He told of a school friend who was at Eastchurch for a short while awaiting discharge on medical grounds. It was here that this man had met an Irish Warrant Officer who had evaded capture after being shot down and at one point during his escape had been hiding in a cupboard while German soldiers were in the room. On reaching the safety of England he refused to fly again. When informed that he would be stripped of rank he threatened to send a list of Resistance helpers to the German Embassy in Dublin. He was gambling that the Board would not realize he was bluffing. It was a successful ploy. He retained his rank.

More than a quarter of a century after the end of the war I was contacted by a former bomb-aimer friend who had read *The Eighth Passenger*. We had lost touch with each other not long after he had been posted to 622 Squadron and I had gone to 218 Squadron. He was now a detective sergeant in the C11 branch of New Scotland Yard. We met again and during the course of conversation he told me of how he had been suspected of lacking moral fibre.

After flying eight or nine operations he had felt tired, listless and without energy. Everything he did needed a great effort and his skin had developed a curious yellow tinge. After returning from his eleventh bombing mission over Germany he had vomited violently. He decided that, for his own sake, and for the sake of his crew, the time had come to report sick.

The Medical Officer had listened attentively to my friend's account of his symptoms and, at the conclusion had asked, "Do you enjoy flying?"

The answer was an unqualified "Yes". The medical officer did not accept this affirmative. "I don't think you do," he had said, "I think you're frightened of flying and that's the reason why you've gone yellow. There's nothing else the matter with you."

Shocked and speechless, my friend had left the room.

He continued flying on operations. The navigator in his crew who had a little medical knowledge diagnosed jaundice and recommended the sick man to avoid eggs, milk, cheese and alcohol. The navigator, and others in the crew, looked after my friend as best they could, making sure he had as much rest as possible and taking such burdens as they could off his shoulders. Or rather, all the crew nursed and looked after him except for the wireless operator. After a bad thirteenth trip over enemy territory the wireless operator was afflicted by the "twitch", a word which described constant involuntary muscle contractions of the face. He felt unable to complete the remaining seventeen operations of the crew's tour. He went LMF, was stripped of rank and posted far away.

However, my friend remained steadfast, slowly recovered his strength and, with his crew and a new wireless operator completed the mandatory thirty sorties. Harsh and incompetent though the Medical Officer had been, he had by his attitude achieved a financial saving to the country's exchequer by not taking my friend off flying duties.

In *The Right of the Line* (Hodder & Stoughton, 1985), a masterly account of the RAF in the European War, 1939-45, John Terraine advances the view that the benefits and privileges of being a commissioned officer helped to maintain a man's morale. In RAF aircrew there was often a mixture of commissioned officers and NCOs. Whilst they faced equal perils in the air, on landing the officers went to better quarters, had a better Mess and were in contact with senior, experienced officers who could give counsel and pass on useful tips. None of these benefits was available to NCOs and perhaps it is not surprising that from the paucity of available statistical evidence it appears that a higher percentage of NCOs than officers went LMF.

Two considerations appear to have impelled the authorities to react most strictly to anyone who wished to opt out of the flying duties for which he had volunteered. The first was that, as is generally agreed, fear can be communicable like an infection. A man whose nerves had gone had to be removed swiftly from immediate contact with his fellows lest he spread the contagion. If the removal is accompanied by the stigma of loss of rank and a forceful reminder that one has let down oneself, one's crew and one's squadron, some waverers might be deterred from themselves going LMF. The other reason for the attitude of the authorities was that many thousands of pounds had been expended on training each member of aircrew and the country was not getting value for money, tax-payers' money, if an airman could be excused further flying duties, with no form of recrimination or punishment, simply because he decided that the going was tougher than he had expected.

Nevertheless, in theory the attitude of the authorities was more compassionate than anecdotal evidence suggests. A correspondent, himself at one time an RAF Medical Officer in the mid-1950s, undertook some research on the question of LMF. In a letter to me he wrote:

"LMF was thought to be of three types:-

(a) exceptional operational stress − usually treated by rest and deployment on a ground job,

(b) flagrant refusal to fly − usually court martial,

(c) loss of confidence in himself or his senior officer.

"When the patient was referred to the M.O. it was for him to decide whether or not there was evidence of medical grounds (physical or mental) requiring definitive treatment with a view to reinstatement of flying status. If in doubt, the patient was referred to a neuropsychiatrist who made a decision following an interview with the man and on the basis of the Commanding Officer's and Medical Officer's reports. The neuropsychiatrist was a specialist in peacetime mental illness but rarely had experience at squadron level. The C.O.'s report was to include comment on courage, sense of duty, perseverance and endurance, both physical and mental. Bearing in mind that all men have different qualities, in theory the report was to assess if the man was performing to the best of *his* ability.

"Those cases referred at the 8-12 trip and past the 24 trip stages were considered to have a more favourable prognosis. Initial failures and extreme stress reactions at any time seemed to have a less favourable outlook. Extraneous factors of significance were considered to be calibre of Commanding Officer, quality of the briefing, and judicious leave periods, or courses."

In recent years technological advances have made the seven-man bomber crew redundant. Jet aircraft have replaced the piston-driven bombers of World War II. Aviation medicine has become more sophisticated. It is unlikely that the accusation of lack of moral fibre will ever again be used to make an airman a reprehensible outcast. When, in 1991, I was discussing the Gulf War with Group Captain Leonard Cheshire VC he told me that there was a strong possibility that if the war had continued flyers in the bomber squadrons would have refused to bomb undefended targets. He didn't think they could be accused of going LMF. In the 1939-45 war it would have been different. Anyone refusing to bomb Dresden or other poorly defended or undefended targets would almost certainly be categorized LMF. Possibly the difference in outlook indicates a measure of progress, although it has to be said that the Gulf War was not, for the British airmen involved, a matter of national survival. The 1939-45 war was, and brutal though the methods of the authorities may sometimes have been, perhaps they had little alternative.

(7) Rowland Mason, a rear gunner on the squadron, wrote to me saying he remembered the Witten raid clearly. He recollected that at briefing we were informed that "north of the Ruhr 140 Lancasters were to slip down the back of the Ruhr and pay Witten a surprise visit. ...The Mustangs and Spitfires were already jettisoning their extra fuel tanks preparing for the oncoming scrap when I saw over to my port beam a formation in oblong block of FW190s. I learned afterwards that four similar blocks had been observed, comprising ME 109s and FW 190s with approximately 40 fighters in each, a total of 160. The flak was still being pumped up and as we neared the target just prior to when the fighters got stuck into the middle of our stream I saw Q-Queenie blown out of the sky, just as Harry McCalla reports. ...It was a real chop day for 218 Squadron. The officer in charge of Flying Control had been electrocuted

whilst testing the Drim system and an aircraftman riding a bicycle along the peri-track in icy conditions had skidded under the wheels of a petrol bowser, both killed, all on the same day as losing two aircraft."

(8) Erkensschwick was, in fact, on the outskirts of the Ruhr mining town of Bochum. After an unsettling delay we took off at 1130 hours to bomb a benzol plant. The authors of the *War Diaries* (op.cit.) classify the raid as a "minor operation", and go on to state, "63 Lancasters of 3 Group carried out a GH raid through thick cloud...No results known. No aircraft lost."

(9) The incident in question is dealt with in greater detail in note 5.

(10) One of my correspondents, a former rear gunner with the Squadron, has added an uncanny dimension to the tragedy of Evers's last sortie. It involves "chop girls", a subject referred to briefly in Part 2 of this book in the chapter devoted to Les. Chop girls were conspicuously unlucky in their relationship with close male friends or lovers. Their men would, more often than not, go missing in action and once a woman acquired the reputation of being a chop girl she was usually shunned by aircrew who, at the best of times, were a superstitious bunch.

On our squadron there was such a woman who I remembered as having laughing eyes and being quite pretty. But, opinions on physical attractiveness seldom being unanimous, my correspondent referred to her as being "of about thirty years, dark, but not particularly attractive". She was a cookhouse WAAF who "would try and organize the extra tit-bits" for the crews she favoured. My correspondent went on to say that on the morning of the Cologne raid he was leaving the Mess on his way to the briefing room when he noticed this WAAF standing by the door.

She had said, "Is Mr Evers flying today?" On being told that he was on the battle-order she had said, "Oh, I wonder if he'll want his flying jacket" and had glanced towards the peg where Evers's jacket hung. My correspondent said he'd mention this to Evers, whereupon she replied, "Yes, tell him I'm looking after it for him," and she took the jacket from its peg and hugged it to herself. When told about this, Evers had said he had deliberately left the jacket in the Mess as he didn't want to use it that day. He was never to wear it again.

Another correspondent informed me that before the war Evers had held a short service commission in the RAF but had been cashiered for reasons unconnected with his flying. On rejoining the RAF in 1939 he was not commissioned but ironically his promotion came through posthumously. He was listed not as Warrant Officer Evers on the "Missing presumed killed" list but as Pilot Officer Evers. He had finally been forgiven for the offence for which he had been cashiered so many years before.

In July, 1992, I received a letter from a former navigator with 218 Squadron, Jim Jeffrey. He added a strange postscript to Evers's last flight. Apparently Evers had been given an extra navigator for this sortie, a F/Sgt F.J. Norton. Presumably as Evers was to lead the stream of 153 Lancasters of 3 Group on the attack on the Gremberg railway yards at Cologne the Vicar had thought he should have two navigators. I can think of no other reason why on this disastrous trip there was literally an eighth passenger. Amazingly Norton survived while all the others perished.

In October, 1992, a memorial was unveiled at Chedburgh in Suffolk in remembrance of all those airmen (including Evers and his crew) who had been killed while based at RAF Chedburgh. It was here that I met Mr Norton and heard from him what he could recall of his miraculous survival. When Evers's leading Lancaster had been hit by flak Norton had sustained a blow to his head. In addition flak fragments lodged in one of his arms. The aircraft dropped about 10,000 feet before Evers managed to get it under control. The Lancaster was hit again and all Mr Norton can remember is a moment when he was aware of falling through air. He may have been concussed by the blow to his head and had either baled out or been helped out by others in the crew. He must have instinctively pulled the parachute ripcord. He knew nothing more until he came to and found himself in a roadside cafe. The police were sent for and he was taken to the local police station. While there, he learned that the bodies of the remainder of the crew had been found. They must have baled out when the stricken Lancaster was too low. Mr Norton was sent to a prisoner of war camp where he remained for the rest of the war in Europe. He still cannot recall anything but the bare outline of events mentioned above.

(11) For at least one crew the trip to Hohenbudberg was not "fairly uneventful". A correspondent who should have flown on this operation but had been temporarily grounded because of "ear trouble" told me that his crew had gone to Hohenbudberg with a spare bod air gunner and had been shot down over the target. There had been no survivors. Without a crew my correspondent had been obliged to finish his tour as a spare bod himself.

(12) Non-commissioned officers who had exceeded the norms of conventional behaviour in the Mess, or some public place, or who had put their crew at risk through incompetence, could expect to be sent to the "Aircrew Refresher Centre" at Sheffield. Here they lived in fairly Spartan conditions in barracks and were subject to rigorous sessions of physical training as well as having to attend lectures. If they failed to respond adequately to the corrective regime they would be regarded as unfit for further aircrew duties and would be transferred to the army or sent to work in the coal mines. One didn't hear about the disgrace of being sent to Sheffield. I first learned of the punishment shortly after joining the squadron. A flight sergeant navigator billeted in a neighbouring Nissen hut was miserably awaiting his posting to Sheffield. Through miscalculation of courses he had taken his crew to bomb a point at least twenty miles from the prescribed target.

(13) As no squadron crews had been lost I assumed that all aircraft "returned safely". I was wrong. J.C.W. Boorman, a fellow bomb-aimer on the Squadron, wrote to tell me that "we lost two engines over the target and had a rather hectic flight back as we couldn't feather them and consequently lost a great deal

of height, eventually landing at Juvincourt in France. Here we had to leave the Lanc, J-Jig, and hitch a ride back." Mr Boorman went on to say, "I do remember being told at briefing that Dresden was full of refugees and that bombing it would be a great help to the Russians....The idea being that the refugees would flood out of Dresden and any other large towns, who heard about it, and jam all the roads for miles."

Two aircraft crashed in France after the Dresden raid. The other aircraft belonged to 115 Squadron and was piloted by Flying Officer Edward Slogrove. It crashed in a field at Haveluy, in north-eastern France. All the crew were killed. Some forty-seven years after the Dresden raid I received a letter from F/O Slogrove's sister. She is anxious to trace anyone who might have known him.

(14) Until recently the pilot of this aircraft, Pete Dunham, had flown with our squadron, but on the Wesel raid he was flying for the first time as the Commanding Officer on 90 Squadron based at Tuddenham. His former crew were taken over by the Vicar and Dunham went to Wesel with an entirely new crew. Recently promoted to Wing Commander, popular and highly regarded, he had already completed three tours of operations; two as an air gunner and one as a navigator. On this, his fourth tour, he was a pilot. It was his eighty-seventh sortie over enemy territory and he was very unlucky to be killed on such an easy raid. The rear gunner of a Lancaster flying immediately behind Pete Dunham's wrote to me, "My hands were shaking with fright, remembering the raid on Wesel, when you mention a Lanc blowing up. Well, we flew straight through the debris, and the remains, my rear turret was filled with smoke. I yelled like mad thinking we were on fire, another Lanc was close behind, almost in our slipstream, I can only conclude this was you."

(15) An account of this raid appears in *Bomber Squadron* by Martyn R. Ford-Jones (William Kimber, 1987). A bomb-aimer, Pat Russell of 15 Squadron, was interviewed by the author. It is clear that, like 218 Squadron, crews of 15 Squadron were much concerned at being routed right through the heavily defended

"Happy Valley" of the Ruhr in broad daylight. Pat Russell stated: "We were miles from the target when we saw the box-barrage of ack-ack bursts. The sky was cloudless and the squadron was getting shot up; every aircraft sustained some damage. Planes could be seen peeling off and parachutes floating down into a large area of smoke and fires..." Russell's aircraft was hit just as he was releasing the bomb load, and the starboard engine set on fire. Fortunately the fire was doused by the Graviner fire extinguisher and the crew returned safely to base on three engines with a Spitfire as escort for part of the journey.

(16) When the Rhine was crossed on 23 March 1945 by the British First Commando Brigade, Wesel had been so saturated by bombing that the town was eventually captured at a cost of only thirty-six casualties. At least, this was the cost to the Allied Forces. Of the view from the other side the authors of *The Bomber Command War Diaries* (op. cit.) write: "Wesel claims to have been the most intensively bombed town, for its size, in Germany. 97 per cent of the buildings in the main town area were destroyed. The population, which had numbered nearly 25,000 on the outbreak of war, was only 1,900 in May 1945."

(17) The raid which the Vicar thoughtfully spared us was on Dessau in East Germany. The town was devastated and eighteen Lancasters lost.

(18) Thanks to information from ex-members of 218 Squadron and others I have obtained fuller details of this tragic loss. On 24 April, 1945, a force of just over 100 Lancasters was being sent to bomb the railway yards at Bad Oldesloe, a town between Hamburg and Lübeck. It was early in the morning when Nicky and his crew took off down the airfield's long runway. During the take-off the Lancaster, J-Jig, lost power on the port side, crashed on to the WAAF site, and burst into flames. But the crew were not killed instantly, as I'd been previously told, but were scrambling out onto a wing when a bomb exploded killing them all. The WAAF site was evacuated and, when the fire

had cooled down, the cookie was defused. Subsequent theory on the disaster was that one engine had failed during take off and the flight engineer, when he had tried to feather it, had feathered the wrong engine, thereby making two engines useless. A take-off on two unserviceable engines, and with a full bomb load, had proved too much even for a Lancaster.

(19) Unknown to me at the time, and not realized until the crew had a reunion in 1983, was the fact that after the Dresden raid Les had given his navigator's chart to Paul as a souvenir. How he managed to do this, I have no idea. All charts should have been handed in. It was the only chart of Les's to be preserved. From the times marked on the chart it is evident that we must have arrived on target just after the master-bomber on the first attack left and before the second master-bomber came on the air. It is clear from David Irving's *The Destruction of Dresden* (William Kimber, 1963) that, owing to the impossibility of identifying the aiming-point because of the violent fire-storm sweeping the city, radio contact with the main bomber force was lost for some minutes while the second master-bomber and his deputy conferred on an alternative marking tactic. According to Les's chart we were over Dresden during these minutes. The radio silence was not therefore, as I had assumed, because the second master-bomber had been killed.

Alexander McKee, in his book *Dresden 1945: The Devil's Tinderbox* (Souvenir Press, 1982), used a number of excerpts from *The Eighth Passenger* and commented: "Miles Tripp wrote that there was no sound of the master-bomber on R/T controlling the attack. Perhaps Miles was deaf in both ears as Nelson was in one eye." The comparison with Nelson was probably meant to be complimentary, but I don't care for it, and it is not true. Had there been a master-bomber on the air it is most likely I should have obeyed instructions. Otherwise how could I explain a contrary action to Dig and the others? Have a moral debate while over Dresden? As it was, I was able to do quietly what I thought was right. This may seem a trivial matter but it is important to me, and I told Mr McKee as much when I had the opportunity to meet him.